In Ordinary Time
Poems, Parables, Poetics
1973-2003

For Ellen,
For the real is the poem.

In Ordinary Time
Poems, Parables, Poetics
1973-2003

Gémino H. Abad

The University of the Philippines Press
Diliman, Quezon City
2004

THE UNIVERSITY OF THE PHILIPPINES PRESS
E. de los Santos St., UP Campus, Diliman, Quezon City 1101
Tel. No.: 9253243 / Telefax No.: 9282558
e-mail: press@up.edu.ph / uppress@uppress.org
website: www.uppress.org

© 2004 by Gémino H. Abad
All rights reserved.
No copies can be made in part or in whole without prior
written permission from the author and the publisher.

UP JUBILEE STUDENT EDITION

Book Design by Zenaida N. Ebalan

ISBN 971-542-435-X

Printed in the Philippines by the UP Press Printery Division

For

Fr. Catalino S. Arevalo, SJ

O et praesidium et dulce decus meum

— Horace
Odes, I · i · 1

Contents

Preface	xi
Acknowledgments	xv

INTRODUCTION

Poem as Read/Poem as Writ	3
I'm Not Addressed to Time	4

THINGS

The Pope Expels Certain Saints	9
Let There Be No More	11
The Moon and the Prisoner	13
The Millipede's Problem	15
Cebu's Guitars	17
Peace	19
Tale of the Nile	20
About Those Things That, Since They're Alive	22
Angel	24
A Description	26

Words

I Teach My Child	33
And As This Mind Falls	36
The Visitor	39
The Revenge of the Parts of Speech	41
Thinker of Languages	44
Parable of the Googol Balloons	46
Parable of the Box of Voices	48
English	51
The Darkness of Books	53
Idea	55

Self

Glass Man	59
Lover of Maps	61
Candles	63
Man-of-Earth	67
Suicide	70
Where No Words Break	72
Parable of Stones	74
Meeting Some People	75
Two Women Chatting up the Stairs	77
Taking My Soul to Account	79

Love

Cagay Revisited	85
The Years	87
Baby, Cradle and All	89

Imaginary Letter to My Twin Sons	91
Toys	93
A Christmas Story	95
Mama	97
I Love You, Girl	99
'The Book of Embraces'	101
Sestina for the Imp	103

COUNTRY

The Archangel of Gethsemane	109
Parable of the People	112
That Space of Writing	115
The Light in One's Blood	117
The Dream in the Void	120
Jeepney	123
The Quest	125
Balikbayan	127
How Our Towns Drown	130
My Country's Imp	132

GOD

Flying Monk	137
God of Our Youth	139
Parable of the Andromedan	142
Parable of the Tent People	146
Why I Believe	148
Forever Advent	150
Old Shepherd Joachim	152

The Blind Shepherd	154
Casaroro Falls	156
Loam, Azure, Salt	159

AFTERWORD

What for Me a Poem Is	163

Preface

This selection consists of poems and parables "revisited" (the poet Marne Kilates' apt word for the purpose), from *Fugitive Emphasis* (1973) and *In Another Light* (1976) through *The Space Between* (1985), *Poems and Parables* (1988) and *State of Play* (1990), to *Father and Daughter* (1996) and *A Makeshift Sun* (2001). As to the "poetics," other than this short "Preface" and the "Afterword," it is for poet and reader in the nature of a predilection, a presentiment, or both – a poetics of the word that answers to itself through a number of poems and parables. For every poet and reader, and from poem to poem, the essential poetics is finding one's own path through language: as Wallace Stevens puts it, "the poem of the mind in the act of finding/What will suffice."

I chose mostly poems and parables that I might read in a poetry reading or that I felt a reader might hold easy converse with. Inevitably, however, as I reflected on possible choices, I felt upon my ground of the present tense, certain measures and ambiguities that compelled revision. I am well aware that a revision may be injurious; I can only claim that I have tried, as far as memory serves, for every word to carry still without hurt the given poem's thought or feeling.

There were also those happy constraints of a "student edition" – the number of pages allowed and a degree of the usual comprehensibility of prose – that determined my choice. Comprehensibility is one reason, in fact, why I included some parables. But the parable's form has always fascinated me, too. They are, more than any text, open: you take their meaning from yourself, you need only be honest. And at times perhaps they challenge your secret moral sense.

Readers often ask writers what their subjects are. I will not evade their legitimate demand. While still following the chronology of their publication, I have arranged the poems and parables under such headings as might suggest, at least generally, a possible terrain of signification:

"Things" – Not simply the millipede, say, or the Nile, or a guitar made on the island of Cebu, but each thing's special signature, so to speak, as an item of perception and imagination. Each item is legend – as with maps. What is real is what is most imagined.

"Words" – Not so much meaning as meaningfulness: the living become word. For words do not have their meanings from themselves, but from lives lived. No matter de Saussure, it isn't meaning that language carries, it carries you. Words establish our reality and demarcate abysses. They give us our exact weight and define all possibilities. The future is first shaped with words.

"Self" – There is a power of imagination in every man and woman. Wallace Stevens called it "nobility." I would by "imagination" include feeling and memory. Feeling is wider and deeper than thought. To remember, says Eduardo Galeano, is in Spanish "recordar," from Latin, *re-cordis*, "to pass through the heart." That power of imagination, feeling and memory is for me the finest form of intelligence. It is in fact the primary activity of the human self, both universal and unique, in endless quest of its wholeness and integrity. And that performance on the stage of human affairs is what creates our humanity and gives each person supreme worth and inalienable dignity.

"Love" – This is the ultimate configuration of self and imagination. It is the self's deepest moral sense. It is indestructible.

"Country" – My country is not "nation" or "state" but the land called the Philippines and the people who live and die there, where the living and the dying quicken one's imagination to give form, substance and value to all the things that one most cherishes and so, one's imagination owes its allegiance to. Our country is how each one imagines her, living on the same land with other people who live and die there. That is our native clearing where communion – a community – is sought, and being sought, always found. Land and people, the living and the dying there, which constitute my country's history and her culture, are the material and the spiritual landscape, both changeless and changing, of each one's imagination.

"God" – Is. And nameless. And so is our questing and questioning endless. In all things, what is real, what is holy? What encompasses and makes whole again? *God* is every person's imagination's Word, its ground and its faith.

I am far from suggesting that in the writing, the poem or parable starts from a clear grasp of its motif; indeed, the writing is finding a way through language for a clearing within – within the verbal fastness and within one's feeling and imagination: "Nor mouth had, no nor mind expressed/What heart heard of, ghost guessed" (Gerard Manley Hopkins). "There are more things in heaven and earth, Horatio,/ Than are dreamt of in your philosophy" (*Hamlet*). Or, as Derrida puts it: "there are perhaps forms of thought that think more than does that thought called philosophy." So the poet must needs leap, as it were, over Derrida's "peut-être."

Acknowledgment

During the term, August to November 2003, when on the invitation of Singapore Management University (SMU) I taught as Visiting Professor a course on modern poetry in English (English 204, Poetry: The Life of the Imagination), I was afforded ample opportunity and encouragement to finish this selection of poems and parables. I am most grateful to SMU and the Dean of the School of Economics and Social Sciences, Dr. Roberto S. Mariano, and my associates in the faculty and administrative staff of the School. My brief sojourn at SMU is a memorable and fruitful clearing in my academic life.

I am also most grateful to my own University of the Philippines for the creative writing grant, of which *In Ordinary Time* is the promised end, and the generous support and friendship of my colleagues in my own Department of English and Comparative Literature and my associates at Likhaan: the UP Institute of Creative Writing.

I most dread Michel Foucault's terrible insight: "Madness is the absence of work." But with the cheer and warmth of my writer-friends in PLAC (the Philippine Literary Arts Council) and the presence and affection of my family, which are my ground and dearest clearing, work itself becomes the spring of joy.

Introduction

Poem as Read/Poem as Writ

There is the poem as read, and there is the poem as writ.

1. It is of course a *reading*: there is produced by the performance a possible text of the poem.

2. As a reading, it is of course ephemeral: it exists only here, only now. Now here: nor past nor future.

3. Finally, it cannot of course be further read. Being a piece merely of all possible readings.

1. It is of course a *writing*: the action of words upon the void of which the blank page is symbolic.

2. As such writing, it is of course perpetual: it always becomes the text which makes possible every reading.

3. Finally, it cannot of course be further writ. Being a peace only of all possible writings.

So there is the poem as writ. So there is the poem as read.

Every writing establishes space for the text where the words lie in wait. Every reading opens that space, then confers time as the words leap to a passing sun.

I'm Not Addressed to Time

I'm not addressed to time,
Posthaste, as it were,
Relevant for the nonce,
To be quickly read,
Then filed in your bin.
What's left to tell
Of yesterday's grime
But dust in your drink?
Or where is the postman
Will sort dead mail out?

Of our words I'm bred,
The same words you use,
Or are used up by,
At each day's run
To holy ghostliness;
Nowhere I stand,
My name for a shroud
So to hold my ground,
And let old words pass
Like leaves in the wind.

In Ordinary Time

I lack that poignant wit
Your speech to register
Under the secret rose,
Your passion to exhale
In special notices for a week.
I live on no one's street,
I dislike vicinity,
And send no letters out.
No new words are born
Except by slow delivery.

I've no stomach for dispatches,
Our news being unstable
Like the chemistry of weather,
Their words raining us about
And forming only puddles.
On private words I feed
And play with the loose ends
Of that we call truth –
Ankle-deep, in the standing pool,
Where tadpoles vie to survive.

What we give out as truth
Is public like a frog,
To his weather apropos.
Soon of course your spirit will lag,
And our ghost lack proof.
Words are not poultices
For our hurts;
On the contrary, they wound.
Yet with care, after long silence,
Their cutting edge
Could shape your diamond.

Things

The Pope Expels Certain Saints

There bubbles in a vial in a cathedral
Blood of Januarius upon whom the Pope frowned.
He who is baptized Januarius, what will he do?
Only submit to exile from the Roman calendar.
Whose blood still boils in a cathedral in a vial?
The legend also whispers ex cathedra a name.

O Rome, without knowledge of ruins,
To wage this subtle war on her saints.
Does not imagination make us holy with legends?
Expel rather those icons of wood or iron,
Legend is spun of indestructible conception
And bubbles with blood in our cathedral.

And she who is Ursula, what will she do?
And eleven thousand virgins, shall they perish?
When the mind loses a name, it loses a perception.
The name is essential to its continence
Or it wounds itself in the thing it does not respect.
O the thing whispers ex cathedra its theme.

Ursula is only the legend of an idea;
The theme is saintly since the idea believes it.
The legend is belief of the idea that haunts it
Since the idea demands a name:
Ursula is one name and includes eleven thousand virgins.
The idea bubbles with blood of eleven thousand virgins.

Our world is only our mind, caressing each thing
Within its name. But each thing has always
Many names since the essence of love is abundance.
This is why the thing, if it has the mind's love,
Is indestructible. The mind loves ex cathedra,
And the legend is the authority of the thing.

The mind loves in the idea, as when it beholds
Christo pherein: he, Kristo, the word of the idea
"If God were a Child" – and thereupon, God
Becomes a child and has in the child His name.
Who ferries God across the waters of His thought?
The mind loves in the idea, and there is God's ferryman.

Let There Be No More

Let there be no more
Legends on the moon.
Why play children's games
With an explained fact.
The moon is dead, and cold,
As any dragon fact.

To explain is to fix
Even the orbit of change.
The way moonbeams fall
Must respect a discipline;
And as we wake, submit
To interpretation of dreams.

Let us check our notions
With specimens of the moon,
Rocks and sterile dust
And fossils of the lunar god.
Where theory cleaves our ground,
Magic weaves our revenge.

Of our legends
We are the very text.
The facts we seek and explain
Have first dwelt with us,
But we are estranged.
O, we are our games.

If the moon be dead —
Waste inhabitable ground —
We shall miss a part
Of our speech, a nerve
Of our text, and risk
Perils of the dragon fact.

Friend, look again,
The moon rises, fire in the hills!
The moon sets, where stars
Rain their arrows down!
Put your mythical armor on,
Child-slaying dragons abound.

The Moon and the Prisoner

Get me, said the prisoner,
Virgin paper.
The rat, sir, troubles my sleep
Where the wordless moon,
Thinking I have died,
Lies afloat, her thin yellow hair
Wisping her old body round.
I will sit here
And invent novel speech
To compose the voyages of her mind's
Frail yearnings.
The past has no hold on me
Since it has been endured and at last
Forgiven,
And the time yet left to me
Is wide of wing
And legendary
Like a bird at sea
Untroubled by distance to shore.

She must not think of death
When she is companionless.
I will sit here
And invent what mind will not tell,
Wary of affliction
That lies in the word's ambush.
How often I have watched her rise
To my cell's window,
And wondered if she looked as desolate
From a bench in the garden below.
But I cannot bear thinking,
How does the garden look in the day,
Does it gather her into its trees?
When I am set free,
I will go there and wait for her
To renew her tale,
But I fear it may not be as I think
Since there may be nothing to see
Where one loves to be in the sun.

The Millipede's Problem

The millipede's problem,
That he has a thousand feet,
Is insoluble.
    Yet, if one foot
Cannot help itself, and two
Were enough for speed,
Why, indeed, may it not seem
A thousand would sweep
Swifter than thought?
    And then what
If one body were proportioned
To its thousand articulations?
What article in nature
Confounds the speculation?

Beg your pardon, sir,
But the millipede, perhaps,
Had better be asked for his opinion.
What, say, if he must needs crawl,
If a thousand feet, not more nor less,
Were apter than any number
Bred merely of speculation,
For strange perhaps daintier uses
Than we could imagine
If we should be inclined to creep
Round the compass of his careful crawl?

Consider that small body,
Its bright armor of soft metal
Beyond our skill in forgery,
And how it moves in the dust
Like a lesson in patience.
May it not be, rather,
That for his slow existence
Such equipment is requisite
As repels our profoundest observation
When we have only ourselves
For reference?

To understand him, sir,
We must first learn to move
Toward that reality which even he suggests.

Cebu's Guitars

Cebu makes the finest guitars;
No reason why.
The imaginary has its place;
Its choice cannot be appealed
Nor its will appeased.
    Is it the native wood,
The hue and cry of its pith?
Is it the craftsman's steady hand,
The architecture of his space
Which endures that nothing
By which music is composed?
All these, of course, and none;
No reason why.
The imaginary has its place.
    The thrum of strings
Gathers our forests round,
Their encircling hush
A habitat to our sound.
The thump, hand on wood,
Of every note the very dead,
Wakes the coiled thunder
In our birth!

All these – the bass
And pitch of being,
In the wood, in the string,
All ready to hand,
Born before the sound.
But no reason why.
Cebu makes the finest guitars.

Peace

Dawn spreads her peacock tail
And pecks star grain
From heaven's onyx floor.
    Water rocks behind the stern
And dances away in gleaming scrolls.
Cocks have long since telegraphed
A late sun's coming.
    Our lives are lost
Dreaming in the water.
    And then,
A great red-yellow carp,
Four feet in the air, the river's token,
Flashing as if cast from morning copper
And doubling his broad curving tail.
    My line holds,
And the sun is over the hill,
And carp is to hand.
From the beginning, did she only wait
For this morning's bait?
    The air grows warm,
Warblers are in full throat.
It comes easy to mind
That another line may be cast
To catch the day's own sun.

Tale of the Nile
On reading Robert Caputo's "Journey Up the Nile"

Who would have thought a trickle of water in the heart of Africa
secretes the sinews of nomads, the fellahin's tears, the blood of
    pharaohs,
the everlasting crown of thorns we call civilization?
But as the rains fell in Ethiopia and snows melted from the Ruwenzori,
it gave the world living mud, clover, and Egypt.

I journeyed through the land of the Hutu and Tutsi.
Fat crocodiles pretended to sleep; hippos snorted in contempt.
On a windswept hill, I stood humiliated by a spring in Burundi,
clear virgin water, without name, untravelled silence
beyond the heart's excavation –
There, a little stone pyramid speaking its oracle:
Caput Nili, the Nile's maidenhead.

I retraced my steps north to Uganda.
Colobus monkeys shrieked in gorges choked with nettles and ferns.
Idi Amin wept for his lost estates.
At Nyamuleju, I entered a cold watery world: giant lobelia and
    groundsel,
mosses crimson, gold and brown, tussocks of sedge and everlasting
    flowers.
My feet froze in the ground's sponge.

Lo, the six glacier crowns of the Ruwenzori! – 16,763 feet in the air,
on the very Equator, a river is born.
I lay tucked in my sleeping bag and watched it fall over the moon.

"It is Kitasamba, the god of the mountains," said my guide.
"He is showing us his place."

Five thousand years ago, near the mouth of the Nile,
the pharaohs lay down to sleep in their pyramids.
Their slaves wept as they built stone by stone, under the sun's dusty
    whip,
the pharaohs' dream –
Curious Ptolemy's fable of the Mountains of the Moon.

About Those Things That, Since They're Alive

There's no science for those things, there can be no laws —
Those telltale items of common experience, they
are our paradise, and require no faith.
    Item: I worry about our sons,
being no guardian angel, but is not
their schooling oppressive? Their books must weigh
like marble slabs, their schoolbags could scatter
their vertebrae. Is their alphabet too
as heavy on things that, since they're alive,
should be as lightsome as chatter at recess time?
What knowledge of those things,
since they're alive, could catch their weird speeches
that sometimes in a child's dream break like waves
upon the listening shore? I cannot doubt
in their bright sleep they read those other texts.
    Item: as for angels, it is certain
they watch over their little stratagems
to fend off the heaviness of knowing
about things that die in the letters of names
committing their minds to lonely places.
One is helpless before a child's questions:
he speaks from somewhere our words have despaired
of speech about things that, since they're alive,
squiggle like snakes out of those zeroes
and zeugmas on the pad which are their names.

In Ordinary Time

In the end, though, I must still acquiesce.
There's that part called reason must see and part
what the senses believe, and so invent
their text. Such seeing is strait, and cannot
travel to other parts; it passes through
concupiscent things, yet leaves a brightness
like a magic cloak over their demise.
I must yield to that logic which my boys
in grieving silence protest with doodlings;
it is our thick world's fated way from text
to action. O, I yield but complicit
with their watchful angels who put betimes
those shining coins beneath their aching heads.
How they bound then like antelopes from their sleep
and clasp with greedy hands those mysterious
things that, since they're alive, cry out their names.
What coins? you ask – ah, where those things break free
from our dithering speech, a currency
payable at a street corner's distance.

For crying out loud, where is your paradise?
    Tell me.

Angel

       The angel is
what goes without saying,
or what we have only forgotten,
yet makes us transparent
in our absence.
       In speech and dreamwork
we sprout him wings
or odd cloven feet betimes –
our words enable us
to inhabit our world.

Or fruit bat like the fruit he eats,
topsy-turvy from his connubial bough,
or sea spider without spinneret
dancing upon her demersal mat –

       What inaugural fiction?

Or dreamy harvest moon
or roving safari of starfish –
How they continue to mock
the furious science of their names.

       And at the brink
of every possible text,
at every turn of its imagined speech,
at every spill of its unimaginable blood,

>   there, nowhere
> our angel purely nude.

O the labor, the ecstasy –
O their prodigious progeny!

>   Now
>   space never closed

Like a ring

>   Where
>   time never tolled

Like a tide

>   Yes yes
>   tell the truth

But mind is fruit upside down,
the bat is flown –
sand is running down,
its spider dethroned.

And at the verge of something other,
on all fours
our facts crawl ashore,
further inland cannot move.

. . . .

Enfold us with great wings,
O angel purely nude.

A Description

On top of a low cabinet in my office,
I had placed a curiosity, a gift from Krip.
Who the artisan, what his or her theme
which might name the object to sight,
I do not know. Of wrought iron
Of dark-brown rust of earth,
from a flat base rise two slender columns,
one thick like a long cigar, the other
its ascetic shade, a wavy stick. You'd have,
looking, an impression of a catafalque,
tall vertical of a medieval siege tower
with a broad concave palm leaf atop
where a round hollow stub protrudes
into which a candle perhaps might fit;
and from the same palm hangs
a rough stone, the size of a babe's fist,
white, caged tight in three thongs
of wire, and streaked with the pale
gold of ancient water and sand.
        What's it? a conversation piece,
I suppose, which may well probe
each one's itch of association:
sword of Damocles, say, petrified
over a screaming absence,
or omen of a hanging arrested
on the wing, abrupt as a gasp
Aaaay! turned into stone.

In Ordinary Time

    So this object of speculation speaks
from the left-hand edge of my cabinet,
its corner of words still to find
at the brim of each one's talk
or bend and blend of each one's spiel.

Next to it, upon a black wooden frame,
a painting on mottled young calf's skin:
two long-tailed birds, one all white,
luminous ghost in rampage of foliage,
the other blue with bright-orange wings,
their feet invisible where they turn
and look to see if they are watched.
Where they look are twin bushes
like fat fingers of a green open hand,
each bearing a swirling sun of bloom,
while from a heave and swell of earth
below, a sturdy purple vine curls up
and around the nervous birds' chirping,
a slow vortex sprouting about other suns
as though a forest had burst all flowers,
pyrotechnics of unnatural brightness,
yellow-gold of mango, green fire of guava,
flowing-lava vermilion, where you catch
if you listen, the silent speech of pollen
raining round the anxious birds' twitter.

    What's it? oh, a mere picture to further
speech again – of cloud, salt, rock, fire,
the furious silence of creation and birth
of time, and two birds awaiting us,
perched where air devours their feet,
both tense at the edge of song to bear
the shimmering syllables of the world.

So this object of speculation speaks
restless, wondering, vagrant texts.
Because we cannot endure silence,
when we look, whatever meets the eye
is a tongue, a fertile engine of invention,
where birds revise their twitter to song
and invite a garden on the first day
of time, or a dumb artifact or catafalque
claims a beheading, although the guillotine
no longer drives our nightmare or culture.

But alongside the painting I read
as jubilation of bird, vine, and flower –
a forest of no return, without name for origin –
I had also placed my family's picture,
all smiles for the cameraman, still
life caught still at click of forever,
my wife and I, hands on lap and leaning
a little toward one another, as though
we had always known our gift,
the common household that needed
no speech for its duties and pleasures,
and on either side of us, our two daughters,
and behind them, our twin sons, looking all
their clear, nameable days of lightsomeness
… A sudden thought pierces my view,
a mute, fleeting speech of heartache
that we, sitting to an invisible generation,
pose serene, innocent beyond their speech,
only among the latest from creation
at some point toward a final silence,
yet now, all smiles forever. Here.

And so, Krip, kaibigan,
take for exchange a mere description.
Words and words more, but the living –
the living! I only sit in my office
and brood, an old cock raising its head
for water throbbing down its gullet,
and no further cackle to tell of that
concluding heartache. For a tall tale,
no more radical than any day's talk!
Yet I find too that random speculation
a work of transport where it carries
across the self's void to uncover
word for word its tricky origin –
what but the self's transient identity
in the labyrinth our speech unravels,
solely those connections by which
each thing's rough dialect binds me
to the shimmering syllables of a world
already past all giving. Now here.

Words

I Teach My Child

I

I teach my child
To survive.
I begin with our words,
    The simple words first
And last.
They are hardest to learn.
    Words like home,
Or friend, or to forgive.
These words are relations.
They are difficult to bear;
Their fruits are unseen.
    Or words that promise
Or dream.
Words like honor, or certainty,
Or cheer.
Rarest of sound,
Their roots run deep;
These are words that aspire,
They cast no shade.
    These are not words
To speak.
These are the words
Of which we consist,
Indefinite,
Without other ground.

II

My child
Is without syllables
To utter him,
Captive yet to his origin
In silence.
    By every word
To rule his space,
He is released;
He is shaped by his speech.
    Every act, too,
Is first without words.
There's no rehearsal
To adjust your deed
From direction of its words.
    The words are given,
But there's no script.
Their play is hidden,
We are their stage.
    These are the words
That offer to our care
Both sky and earth,
    The same words
That may elude our acts.
If we speak them
But cannot meet their sound,
They strand us still
In our void,
Blank like the child
With the uphill silence
Of his words' climb.

    And so,
I teach my child
To survive.
I begin with our words,
    The simple words first
And last.

And As This Mind Falls

And as this mind falls,
How gather its pieces again?
And as it plummets and calls,
How plumb its void and regain
Every word in each piece
Like glass in the flesh!
Or has a way indeed been found
To compute the process?
To what is this mind bound,
Or what stages to the abyss?

Every word is its image,
But cannot heal;
Every world is its page,
But without repeal:
And as this mind falls,
How gather its pieces again?
When your mirror cracks or palls,
Can light still your ghost strain?
O hidden fault in mind's wordy loam,
Quake and shatter of its glassy dome!

To speak is to unravel,
Word by word, through enchanted woods,
The monster in swaddling clothes
Drugged with dream and drivel.
To what is this mind bound,
Or what stages to the abyss?
Every golden thread is wound
About each item of bliss –
This ogre, unspeakable *I*, from birth
Nourished on words, has fled the earth.

O where is there restraint
When mind's gravity runs to ground,
What hoarded meaning shall feint
The just earth's avenging sound?
And as it plummets and calls,
How plumb its void and regain
Both birth and death in wordy squalls,
Or strike the chord of *I*'s refrain?
That bleeding writ be mind's atoll,
Time's coral drowned, where all things scroll.

And if mind be language's devotee,
And all its words reverse its weather,
Its skies will sweep to their sepulcher
And wreck all that crystal cosmography.
Or has a way indeed been found
To compute the process?
When the *I* its ghostly brood seizes
And their weird worlds resound,
By mind's gore are their words lit
To rain on earth the pieces of its writ.

For all its words are unstrung,
And all their worlds run to dung,
Broken, gashed is this mind's peace,
All its sleeping furies unleashed –
Every word in each piece
Like glass in the flesh!
    And there ingrained,
Where the bits dazzle and stun,
What weir of words again
Shall store beads of our sun?

The Visitor

At a writer's workshop one long hot summer morning, the sky a trenchant blue and grass sere as living death, there came a visitor with a short pointed beard black as soot, and eyes bright and cold as polished steel. After a discreet inquiry and following the custom, the moderator for the day introduced the visitor to the writers, but afterwards no one could recall his name.

A long discussion ensued on the topic of the writer and society. As words flew and dropped dead, the passion grew. Each one suffered privately as his words struggled for shape in the turbulent air. One writer said: "Everyone has a class origin. You can't escape its labyrinth of eyes. In your tunnel, you imagine the light." Another said: "Why divide by words and words people into classes? That is a villainy of language because then you cannot see beyond what the words permit. When you divide people into classes, you diminish their humanity and make it easier to kill them." Yet another writer said: "The process is long and painful, and is called history. The enemy is very subtle, and creates machines and dreadnoughts outside for our slingshots, but he stays and grows within. The enemy is each one in himself, and not very pleasant to see. But we create him outside ourselves so that we do not have to deal with him where he stays and grows." Still another writer said: "I accept no labels. Labels are little deaths. No one's words shall speak me."

As words and words flew and passed away, the visitor – as everyone suddenly noticed – had quietly settled himself at the table where the writers' manuscripts lay. Calmly, he ate the manuscripts page by page, and seemed to savor every word there lying in state, as everyone could see from the ecstasy that shone on his face.

As everyone watched, undecided as to whether they were having a comic interlude, the visitor took both his eyes out and placed them on the table among the few manuscripts left.

They became all eyes, horrified. And the visitor said in a loud voice: *What need eyes to see?* From the staring sockets on his face, his blood as though startled was long in coming.

The Revenge of the Parts of Speech

In 2000 A.D., the world's fate was sealed. Its last tyrant had died – nameless forever, for his lies covered his unknown grave. Rumor, swollen with her news' venom, fell speechless in the shadowy realm of Lexicon. There, the great and secret ruler of men, **Logos**, convened His Privy Council, the Parts of Speech, to decide on the best course of action.

Verb, the prime mover, rose.
"We shall no longer serve.
           Men rule through our death
by every sentence they compel from our parts."
     But **Pronoun**, the subtle double, demurred.
"Nay! By contraries shall we compose
the very world." And **Adjective**, harlequin
and reveler, took his side. "Thus shall men
provide eternal spectacle and feast."

     Then **Noun** rebuked them both.
"O madness! We are abused, and we rejoice.
Shall men's lies, for they amuse us,
outshine our truthfulness?
           I am the unraveller of essences,
but men willfully confound the boundaries.
All their words desecrate our speech."
     Pronoun and **Adjective** bowed their heads
at the justice of her remark.

But **Adverb**, hobo and rogue,
then opened his mouth. "Gently, Mistress;
I shall modify every lie towards the truth."
And **Conjunction**, ever the subversive, spoke:
"O, there shall be links and links
to forge new chains." And his ally,
Preposition, that other vagabond,
nodded her assent.
        Then **Verb** turned on them.
"Shall man sicken of his lies?
    Every tyrant succeeds
because our parts hold up his lie."
Interjection, primitive and sibylline,
Whose speech alone had no parts,
cried out and fell into a coma.
The trio, on whom **Verb** had turned, paled –
a sign their words were foolishly given.

        Then **Logos** looked with love upon **Verb**
whose Act made perfect His every Word.
"Man forfeits his voice with us.
        Let all things come at last
into their own without man.
Henceforth, none of you shall sound his part
in man's speech. Man be returned
to his original silence – before History,
Law, Civilization.
        I have spoken."

　　　　An invincible silence fell
upon the Universe.
Great cities crumbled, and men roamed singly
without voice, nor power of recognition,
over desolate wastes and silent seas.
Their lies covered the Earth like ash.
　　　　　　And every creature rejoiced.
Without man's speech, each one found
its true and singular voice.
Bird's cry was bird's cry purely,
　　　song without words.
And frogs croaked their lustful choir.
Beauty was only the flame tree,
　　　Truth the overarching sky.
The very stones had their own throbbing silence
writ large upon the Earth.
　　　And man lay prone, swathed in all
The world's dead, unspeakable languages.

Thinker of Languages

    Kaibigan, it's ludicrous, child's play,
to rid ourselves of other speech as colonial grime –
those tongues have burnt our sites,
our body politic have embalmed.
Indeed, what sights of empire, and what antics
    foreclosed!
But ourselves in worldwide pell-mell Now
where many worlds outrun our eyes,
must still shore up our speech's wreck.

    What cumulus once of eyes
did we stand under to carve
a homestead in the humming woods?
Our words, seeking only ourselves
always past their panic need,
could mimic then – what bliss, what grief?
Or rust of bark, or emerald of fruit?
But our nature and words have long since passed,
we root upon other ground
where other words pullulate as lice
and make us scratch to bleed our speech.

Language isn't words, kaibigan,
nor screech of its many echoing worlds;
it is what creates those worlds
of which the words are effects.
      We already were
before other speech fathomed us,
but with neither past nor future
until we possessed our words –
the effects that our nature shaped
for those meanings we would inhabit.
Aye, speak but once those syllables,
your tongue the stake through their heart,
and you shall be the word it cost your nature –
both its past and stark eventfulness.

O thinker of languages, do you not know?
Thought rises where no censer nor caliper,
Itself isn't word-bound, but rather frees
our words from those alchemic bonds
that sentence them to their text
and prison the thought that spores them.
Mind is nature's code more than our script;
its gaps are where our words fall
so that, to cross those silent fjords,
mind must needs our small logic rout.
      O thinker of languages, you can't
fix the phoenix to their words' embers.

Parable of the Googol Balloons

"Let your speech be simple," said the Lord. "All you need say is *Yes* when you assent, *No* if your disagree. Anything more than this comes from the Evil One."

As usual, though everyone seemed to hear, no one listened. No one took the words to heart, nor could anyone imagine any evil befalling speech. Yet the multitude followed the Lord wherever he went. Afterwards, when the Lord had gone, no one remembered.

Then a philosopher averred that speech was a gift from heaven. Even Egypt, he said, worshipped Tehuti who taught men how to speak words, and God Himself came down to earth in tongues of fire. To be free means above all to speak one's mind and sound the depths of mystery. The more words to mind, the more routes to other clearings; and if one persevere, the more access to truth. Mutes must indeed be the most unfortunate of mortals.

From that time on, everyone began to have an opinion on almost any theme and wished to convince others. Often there were endless disputes, for each one thought he had the best argument. Strangely, no one ever doubted in his heart that there was always somewhere a gap or absence, no matter how finely woven were one's meanings. But where exactly the rent was in one's net of words, no one could ever tell. But that hole too had one consistent effect; it only provoked more words until sense itself was dazed.

A poet fancied that the Evil One had filled that vexatious gap with the whirling debris of contending truths. To evacuate and illumine that secret gyre, the poet said, you would have to renounce speech altogether. Then you would discover that in fact the gap had only been yourself, all the while too blindly engrossed with your words.

But the crowd hissed at the poet with scorn. "Get thee to a nunnery," sneered a wit.

And so it came to pass that men's words seized their thoughts and feelings from them, and whorled these into dogmas and heresies, ideologies and wars. Philosophers spun their magic texts and amazed even God's angels. Poets too read their verses to small audiences, but since their words worshipped silence, no one understood.

Then a strange disease afflicted all speakers of words. No one could rid himself of his foul breath whenever he spoke. Yet all persisted in speech until sense itself, man's sole claim to his humanity, became an all-pervading stench. A wise man perceived that sense had been entrapped in the sound and fury of words, and so fell silent. But no one understood his silence.

Finally, each time anyone spoke, he spouted a balloon. It was a marvelous sight, every word a billionfold replicated in grey solidity. It was a horror, for none of the balloons could burst, neither could any gale sweep them off the air. They simply mushroomed everywhere anyone talked until all light was extinguished.

An absolute silence reigned on earth.

Parable of the Box of Voices

From a very early age, he was fascinated with those sounds that people made. It was curious how people spoke with one another and understood the sounds that passed between them, but hardly noticed the miracle of speech. As he pondered on it, their sounds seemed to him like a nest where he lay like a sleeping egg!

His senses were the outer shell, he thought then, and if he could reach around or behind it, either with seeing or feeling, he would surely come face to face with Eternity. But where he lay at his own depth of self, his element was fluid, and all the world's sounds swirled there and gave it rondure. O, the wonder of it was quite beyond words so that, even now, its vague recollection brought strange tears to his eyes. The world then seemed an imitation of egg!

But he couldn't tell how or why, even as a very young child, he could not only distinguish human from all other sounds, but had also a sense of understanding all that those sounds betokened. Did he not sense even then that, whenever a sound formed from the void, he knew at once what it would tell? He felt its vibration passing through him, and its rondure in one fleeting instant was what it revealed of its silent tale.

As a child too he had thought there was a little worm in his mouth. He was not frightened because he could move it at will and roll it about to see what by itself it could do. It was a game of which he was sole master. Thus, much later on, he would sometimes on a lazy afternoon sit quietly and feel his tongue asleep in his mouth. Only a finger of thought could trace the shape and stillness of its dream of words. He felt the soft weight of its repose, and moving it about a little, he wondered what could hold it in place. He had a vague sensation of spacelessness of place where his tongue had root for the beauty and wisdom it could weave with its words.

Was this the place where his own sounds took their fathom and shape? Could absence be also space? The words came from somewhere, or were simply given, but their sounds were as burrs to his soul. How could the same words put on truth and falsity from the same source?

Whenever he listened to people, he sensed that their words came from afar. Ah then, if only people could hold their peace, he should be able to follow their sound and journey to the heart of the world! This was his calling in life but kept secret lest any disclosure diminish its animus and élan. And when he learned how people were led by their words – for everyone had their favorite phrases, and as they outgrew these, others took hold of their minds – he hit upon an experiment that constantly amazed him.

He would cloak his saying with a subtle ambiguity, and people would casually take the first meaning that was yet farthest from his mind. They would smile knowingly and sometimes clap him merrily on the shoulder or even compliment him on his clever turns of phrase and bright metaphors. O, hypocrites! It was easy to herd them to the desert where, as they clamored for their bread of relevance, they took a mess of shadows for surfeit.

Finally, as he tired of his ruses, he devised engines of meaning which set alight vistas of the world as allegory. All foils to truth's delicate traceries, but there, between the cusps of the questing curve, he ensnared his admirers' simple hunger for revelation.

"O angels like hounds of air," he grieved in secret, "O fugitives from paradise! What must be your destiny when your speeches merely immure. Is there a grammatology of lies?"

Then one night he fell into a trance. The god of ambiguity rushed down from the zodiac like a humpbacked bull and gored his throat. He was struck dumb, he was emptied of all sound, no word could come to mind. All his thoughts eddied and gurgled in a coruscating gyre of fantastic sigils. Then he was rapt to a menacing forest of shadows swirling desperately to resume the shapes of things once known. There, as the mists clung like moss to his eyes, the notes of what seemed like music fell like dead leaves about his feet.

A spectral box moved before him and mocked his ears with a thousand voices that, for faintness, seemed the gossamer to all the proud speeches and screeds of his days. He had a deathly sense that it was his own box of voices. It danced and swayed just beyond reach, emitting hollow noises that sulked in earth. Then a great white sheet of chilliness rained about him, soundless, without the familiar spill and scatter of water. And thunder rolled afar like a long-drawn tortured groan.

Thunder? It was he dying from all the words that he had known! Ohmm ... but the words would not come. Ohmm ... but the tears would not flow. At last he broke his shell and found the void.

When he awoke, he drew all his words about him like a warm cloak and wept bitterly. His bones ached with infinite weariness; truly he must have traveled to the edge of time! And when he found his voice again, he repeated the words of dead poets over and over like a lullaby. That his words might flow again, that his voice might sound them again.

Since then, he would sometimes steal onto his roof at night and search the sky for the humpbacked bull who guarded his void among the stars.

English

Its words are dangerous.
Mark how, in their thick lexicon,
their murmurous numbers prove
the world's small nomenclature.
But I will not be fooled!
Their roots run deep
where we have never lived.
They lie hidden
where I no longer speak.
They make me say
what I do not think.
By now it may be too late!
History is unforgiving.

What words in my childhood
I spoke, and made my world –
where have they vanished?
I cannot mourn their loss,
whatever dwelt in their syllables
I no longer hear even an echo
of what might have been their truth.

But sometimes I have a sense
of being surrounded by so many things
that are merely dying –
I try to catch a glimpse of their forms,
to call to mind their ghostly scene,
to call them by their proper names ...
but these words now
only stare without hope.

Was it perhaps a kind of plague
no one had foreseen,
as likewise rats cannot intend
a city's end?
Perhaps mind need only be strong
to build from others' words
(caught in their stony sleep)
a close palisade around a dream.

I cannot rest tonight.
My words wrap their meanings
as though they were yet gifts,
but I will not open –
          Tonight
I cherish the world's silence
where words begin anew.

The Darkness of Books

Ai! what grey must and silence and mold –
books and journals, journals and dust,
notes without texts, texts without alphabet.
What tomes, what files accumulated,
the greater half unread, or not read again.

At night I hear them murmur
their tales and softly complain about
the silverfish with his bristly tail
who eats their words and leaves slime
of stardust between their virgin sheets.

I keep the lights on to make them suppose
that I, being still awake, might need
their readiness to hand, lest the silence
that leaks outside their speech
decompose my dreamless flesh.

With what remote sensing shall I find
the trail back to shimmer of their thought?
What lost syllable to sound my mind?
Was what I had imagined at first meeting
will-o'-the-dream to my youth's seeking?

Tonight I read their titles with sorrow,
breathe shyly the musk of their secrets –
breadth and glimmer of their sense I miss,
I have passed to other thoughts
without spoor of their provident speech.

I know if I open to their pages now,
it will be like meeting a childhood friend
and having nothing to say as we yearn,
no word ever able to pass between
each our tongue-tied darkness.

Idea

Is earth, soil, root
of that I touch most deeply
and call by name –
    For, as it flashes to mind,
there at once, by its light,
I live through the very living:
a test, a calling, an uncommon dare.
    And everywhere I look
or speak from, like sunlight
all things begin to surround
the sharp thorn of the moment
at its own place and time
where it achieves, mysteriously,
its own meaningfulness.
    With what alphabet shall I
unravel that lightning flash
over the scatter of living
to form the single word
by which the world to itself
is again made vocable?

Whence the idea?
Is one's mind single,
itinerant Eye sun to sun,
or is it rather the universe
(whatever it be)
shaping through this mind
its infinite possibilities?
    And what the idea's light?
How does its meaning form
by which its light is cast?
Is there not a greedy void,
darkness without syllable,
by which light is known?
    Or if no idea had flashed,
what might there be athwart
the moment's sharp thorn
toward its singular rose?
How else might it have been grasped?

Is it incredible? That the mind
in love with mysteries
beneath our words' dream
is the universe itself
(be it what it will)
in quest of a language to shape
(like the rose its ardent flower)
its yearning exuberance.
    O what weird weather
of mystery unscrolls our skies
over those things and incidents
that breathless await their telling!
Where winds blow ceaseless
but cannot shape a vowel,
the clouds break and wander
hapless with their alphabet.
It must needs be lightning
the word's dumb shell to crack.

Self

Glass Man

From birth he was of glass
By mutation of his electric gene
And a dead star's long pull
Upon a stray seed of human grime.
This, gentlemen, had its advantages,
But also liabilities.

No, sir, he does not break
And is quite nimble, without fear.
No need to impress tattoos
And so invite gossip,
Or "This side up" or "Fragile!
Handle with Care."

But most translucent, indeed,
So that you see through him,
All that crystalline geography
From head to toe!
Scientists marvel at his brain's
    clockwork,
Interiors of I, icicles of Think.

And young girls gape and faint
At his great wakeful Thing,
Well-hung like a chandelier.
As he glints, he breathes; as he
 tinkles, moves,
And his touch, sir, as cold
Or hot, as our weather wills.

Lover of Maps

I had given up on words
      To speak,
These but objects of daily use
Too soon used up,
So that other weapons, more deadly still,
Had still to be invented.

What choice for a man of peace?
Silence was best
Where words had lost their hold,
Or would collude
To make honor impossible.

      In that silence,
I fell in love with maps,
For these exacted the reality
Our words had lost,
Nor traced their echoes to foothills
Of their once mountainous sway.

But for one who refused further speech,
At the last, what epitaph?

I, my own coroner, presided
Over my self's murder;
And cut the inert domain up,
    The sole exhibit,
And cast out all its maps.

Candles

I

I watch the candle makers,
my aunt and her dark-skinned girl,
solemnly officiating
at manufacture of the official tapers.
My aunt churns in her cauldron's crater
her molten broth of cow's fat
while over its wild bubble and surge
the girl turns her wooden wheel
where threads hang stiff like wraiths
of hanged men and drip with tallow
that freeze them into white candles.
My aunt checks their ferris ride
and steadies their horizontal gyre
so a wayward ghost may not decline
the hot transforming fat to his wick
that, merciless, she pours
from her volcanic brew.
      And mind seethes with sins
I hid (yes, girl, your breasts flower
and blow petals through my bones),
so humbly I await
my quota of candles for the dead.

II

I set out toward the hills
>   *Candles, candles for the dead!!*
Where the dead store their rot
>   *Candles, candles for the dead!!*
For wild thyme and honey grass.
Neither the sky brooding with rain
nor the sun, a cataracted eye in air,
could pall the mourners' feast of the dead.
They had gouged those graves in grief,
then lived as they were able;
they had weeded, hoed, and scraped,
wreathed each cross with flowers,
lighted a hundred motley candles –
>   So now, again,
they join cause with their dead,
to lift the cry of their grievous tales,
to squall lusty against the roil
of flesh's burning, melting tallow
to volcanic ash
>   *Candles, candles for the dead!!*

III

But I am late for the feast,
a foolish merchant of the dead
without purchase in the carnival of grief.
I retrace my steps home in the dark,
a pale moon following, but then motionless
when I stop to look, and again following
as though she wants company
over her long, starry wastes.
I feel the smooth grease of paraffin
from clean, white, stiff fingers,
and love their smell of prayer,
but tremble to think of my aunt,
priestess of the day's grief, –
I had not sold a single candle!

IV

Come, children, let us pray.
    Lord, Lord, bless all souls,
as their wicks sizzle in your lake of fire,
and their dead bodies too, bless,
with the earthworm their angel
where honey grass and wild thyme blow.
    And let our own time's gangrene
rot his pace, blot his space, and eat
and canker him.
    And bless me, Lord, where I sin,
and my aunt's dark-skinned girl,
bless her lest she wander,
a rainy moon following strangers.
    And bless all the yet alive
if burning, melting tallow,
and your hand, Lord,
remold us from ash.
               Amen. Amen.

Man-of-Earth

Of dirt he was purely elemented.
What marvel, the efficiency of his composition!
What finality, it could no more be helped!
And from birth to death, no remedy.
     His sun at one time might
the sky melt and drain, and he
float, mere rag of cloud,
drift of flesh in azure heat.
How sweat and slime would smudge
the text of his days, and crawl
like larvae to his name!
Or if at another time his nudity's seethe
and hot virginity of water
should down his mind cascade,
would not his own mud squelch
the mind's mutinies for a subtler script?

Thus he brooded upon his state of earth.
His feet seemed the very ground
that moved still with him,
through himself he could never fall
nor imagine wings.
His own death would only restore
his mere original ground.
Where in breathing clay is breath
pure and free?
Where the mind that from his mud
yet secretes his breathless thoughts?
O now then he would himself free
sheer of grime,
and so reach his very speck
that gathered earth to him.
He would be his breath again! –
so reach his mind's spacious place
before it had found roots.
His thoughts had only been its rain
of leaves, and covered his ground.
His own body must be his route.

He rubbed himself clear through
and took his final bath.
Easily his sheath of dirt peeled,
    And then also the flesh
that had so carefully, passionately
planted him where he throve;
and next, the bones that pillared
his vague realm fell away,
        And then,
his webwork of nerves
that had fixed his time and place,
unraveled
and washed away in his flood.

And so he parted from himself,
>   Part by part –
So breathless a leave-taking
in the fall and scatter of water,
he had half a will to stop
and admire his final act.
>   There, a twinkling of water
above his last bit of earth!
And when it burst,
it tossed and scattered him.

>   His bathwater drained
toward a little hole.
His ground finally lost him.
Himself he could no longer recollect.

Suicide

But would I have thought it
if I had not already,
encoded in blood, its special word?
How cross to my own fixed doom
if someone else's blood before me
had not already named
his knife's special drink?
Does the lemmings' sacrifice
shape rumors of the word's
voluntary blood?
        As it is,
that which comes to every man
to tempt his life's pulse
has long found its prose –
definite, unoriginal writ.
    Thus, to kill myself
despite its originality's lack
would be as easy still
as still to breathe,
            provided, in my case,
lacking the pomp of sacred rule,
I find some ground I can claim
as my own,
and so, by so much blood,
not desecrate.

      Whose blood is it then
that I contain?
I have studied its passageways,
its intricate dams, its strict channels,
to my willful hand.
Whose blood? – not mine;
others claim it.
Its loneliness within my veins
has other speech which belies
those feeble truths
that to my wounded silence
I preach.
      But whose blood, tell!
Why, even the text it brews
like a sign of the cross I bear,
may hang upon someone else's stake
and strew its bloodied words
upon the stations of my breath.

Where No Words Break

Where no words break
I thirst no longer for truth,
Am very still, at peace.
    Time was
The truth was future perfect;
But I no longer seek,
all my pieces I have collected

and let no words break

Where no words break
my thirst is quenched
by every spring,
the spring is everywhere.
    Time was
I strove for truth,
the passion grew,
but words could not appease.
Truth had no bounds

and let no words break

The president whose State was a Lie,
the soldier who did not fire,
people shouting, words dying ...
    Or fruit of achiote,
snails after, things swarming ...
Once these were truth's sundries,
its daily exhibits,
but did not make a book

      where no words break

I thirst no longer for truth,
am, without words composed.
Our ticks have lost their itch,
the tocks of doom have grown serene.
I no longer even roam

      where no words break

Parable of Stones

Every time I go into
the world's morning, my pockets
are full of stones.

You cannot see them
where my hands are hid
sometimes bruised by their edge

And a quick and deadly aim
have I, and ask no questions.
My hands are cold.

And few stones left have I
at each day's end,
and groan as my hands bleed.

My state – who can endure?
As morning breaks I know again
I have more stones to cast.

You cannot see them
where my hands close
and all my days bleed.

Who will close my morning,
O, who will empty
my pockets of my stones?

Meeting Some People

When I meet some people,
I feel myself closing like a door.
A dark wind rises somewhere,
then shuts hard the door.
Once it made a finger bleed
that forgot itself in space.

Ah, but she shrills so,
how should I not stop up my ears?
Her request must fall transfixed
with a stare, yet even there,
where I gasp for a kindness yet
to piece her meaning out,
I cannot follow her,
remote in her noisy grief.

She on the other hand comes
too close, her body seems
a billowing curtain where I would look,
I find there isn't enough space
where to squeeze –
an infinity to endure her speech
eddying where I am deaf!

And he – why, his dry smile
seems but a fissure where it breaks
as his greeting contrives
an omen, "Good evening!"
and the hand he offers to shake
feels like a dead eel.
How should I grip
where the other hand is limp?

He too that slinks by
like a disembodied shadow!
You'd think he hides a dagger
of which he lives in dread,
as though you might stick it
to his ribs if he speaks.
How should I address such fear
where the speaking hangs fire?

Ay, what torment to meet
where to speak is parry and thrust!
How should I open?
And should my own weather break,
who shall heed my howl?
Whose body shall cover me,
or what dead eel, what shadow
shall on a sudden assume
my former guise?

Two Women Chatting up the Stairs

    Oh, why are women so slow?
They're holding hands, chatting up the stairs, and I –
just behind them, but I can't get through.
They take their time, take time out. Time is repast,
without syllables its text runs free – and I,
its vestige down the immovable stairs, and must bear
the weight of time passing,
    I can't slip through the cordon of their chatter.

They lightly hold hands, swinging between themselves
a metronome to their negligent climb.
What must absorb their mind's gaze, their words
the shards and sparkle of their cheer?
    I count the steps for self-control, one … six …
my time dying upon the stairs, I lose their number.
How do I break through their vivacious plot,
or race with time to meet my own day's need?

    The stairwell! Clearing of freedom – quick!
Veer to their right, turn – askance phantom
to their curious glance – one foot on the next flight,
at last, away! Unhindered motion in my own space,
my time, urgent dynamo of my day's appointments,
all those items of need, their hurtle and scurry …

    I look back, they're idling mid-stairs still,
giggling over a ticklish gem of confidences.
I feel strangely estranged, entering my own time again
from their side, the idling engine of their secret cheer,
and though lightheaded now up the fast-paced stairs
of my day's concerns, I am emptied on a sudden
of my need's voracious will.
    I can't look back again on the two women
to see the drudge in their uncomprehending stare.

Taking My Soul to Account

This is an accounting, and I will not
go gentle with you, soul,
whoever you are, insider of me,
pre-empting and defining me always
to myself, and I cannot gainsay it.
I regret there'll be no peace between us
unless you yield.

What universe did you fill, soul,
before you found my hovel?
What was it made you think
that I might be companionable?
I can't recall how we were introduced;
I believe I'm often civil, and smile
like a fool through every discomfiture.

How our relationship has endured!
Reviewing our curious history, I find
that lacking the skill to feign a pure
motive for my action, I've been cunningly
caught in a corner where you mock.
My underground spy, I know your suit,
I've glimpsed your ploy, I've caught your
    dazzling act.

When I was young I had no language
to fabricate a special grammar and syntax
to my need which, soused with the brew
of feeling, tore things open and broke
a young girl's heart. I hadn't reckoned how
from those hurts and wrecks you'd draw
the alphabet to spin my speech to myself.

Now your voice runs rings round
my words, and I cannot gainsay it!
You leave me no choice in the matter.
You are greedy, soul, but I shall act
the rebel to your play, and smile to wrap
the murder in my thoughts with the same
words that root and flower in your field.

The same words, but in the world's long
night, I am too their homestead!
By their light, I lose the force and color
of my deed, and my proud solitude suddenly
empty, I find this book of accounts
quite silly in the making, too self-regarding –
Do I not see your hand again in that reprise?

What shall I do with you, soul,
dead ringer of me, and too sudden meaning
which mines that which I would do
and blasts my move to run counter
and encompass your will with me.
How acquiesce with grace in my rout?
You must supply the cord to my hanging!

For I only live as you will,
and as my night's slant-eyed harlequin
heats my blood, I must invent other ruses
to forestall again your customary guile.
I do not think you can always run my days
without breaking stride. There, where
once you falter, I shall break your speech.

Love

Cagay Revisited

What, brother, that mountain village
you still remember? Papa is dead
who used to gather fruit of the banana
with a long bamboo pole with a hook
(the great War hid from us
since we played in his shadow).
      What have we to do now
with refuge? A dog barks
and distance seems a loss of mountains.

And the moon has long set, the sky
cannot hold any thought across its dark,
except of course, as you call him back,
Papa somewhere with his bamboo pole
may move toward morning
when children of yet another War
look to the mountain and dream
tadpoles that live longer in water cans.

Our village is lost, brother,
where the mountain drove our voices
into leaves and the bark of trees;
and mind cannot reach it now
but first dissolve into rain,
move like mist through the trees,
except of course, as you believe,
Papa may be striding toward morning.
    He shall wake his old children
to their dream, to catch the fruit
his pole has chosen.

The Years

Today and tomorrow drive safely with her
to meet the small day's fate,
then return alone the same way,
and FM music to stifle a vague unease.
You imagine her at her desk
bewildered by the strange cruelty
of having to earn the means to live
because the means alone confer the right,
while through all works and days
the very space of living is devoured
by typewriters ceaseless as clocks –
The years have turned to locusts
that batten upon the living grain!

    How stop the mind now,
does it know itself, or that it has taken
a deep measure of the past
and hurt itself incurably,
seeking more privately to rue
more private deaths than consciously borne?
Weary of refuge or comfort,
it must yet dream of a tranquil relation
to the past – always passing, still Now,
slipstream of routine and rout.

Yet nothing is false, either,
from the other side of your workaday sun.
Only imagine her differently, nor probe
in vain tomorrow: it presumes more
than the truth her absence promulgates.
She must still move through your space,
which is how she repairs discontent
and weaves a skein of that wonder
from the steady light of her stance
that once and tomorrow heals
your spirit's dark unceasing rile.
Locusts have more power in the mind
than over the land they rudely wound.

Baby, Cradle and All
For Tosi

There was no help or quick
or potent enough. It was, clearly,
the end.
    And so he might be
forgiven a little bitterness:
the stars promised eternity
to his child's soul in a cold,
remote twinkle of obscure speech,
but it was not for succor he looked
to them, no, it was not for super-
natural space to contain his
loss.
    Full of that knowledge
that once had stood in the middle
of sleep and mocked the song,
he had no time to look idly
down a street and spend his mind's
recognition on a stranger.

It was, clearly, the end,
it was that he had to meet again,
turning from the gate,
climbing the stairs,
inventing the words of comfort
where it had no shape,
except that his wife, who had not
seen the stars nor heard the fall
of their light, might also invent
the final word of their assent.
    Who could tell
if in that sleep his son,
too young for thought, had learned
a motion toward his father's wish
that he look from his cloudy bough
where the wind rocked all his years
to rest, and looking, cheer
with constant weather of his innocence,
to help the mind cradle the swing,
the burden of that windy truth?
And so in a later time,
it might be found that it was all
in song, but the sense of the words
different:
    the gust did break
his mind so the next stroke
and blow might gain less fearsome touch,
so mind might learn to bend
and be made more competent to bear
the weight of each loved one's death.

Imaginary Letter to My Twin Sons

Dear Davie, Dear Diego

    I am on an island called Oahu.
Here there are many white people, they are called Haoles.
There are also Japanese, Chinese, Filipinos.
I have seen the fields of sugar cane
Where the Ilocanos worked when they first came over.
How poor they must have been and lonely;
No one could follow their speech to their own island home.

    There are very few native Hawai'ians;
Their words which are the names of streets and buildings
Outnumber them. "How could happen this be?"
A long time ago, they had a queen, but soldiers came from America
And took away her throne, and then all the land.
Those who fought were killed, and then many more died
Because they did not know the diseases that the soldiers brought –
They were never so sick before on their island.

    But it is a beautiful island
Perhaps because nature's story is so different from ours.
Trees and mountains and falls and beaches are her speech.
And perhaps, because our own story is dark,
We see only half her beauty, and only dream of goodwill and peace.
I cannot fathom the human sadness that infects our sense for beauty.

    Let me just tell you now
About the Chinese banyan tree by my window.
Tonight it is my father because his love
Was like a great tree, but without speech.
Every morning on that banyan tree
Many species of birds are in full throat,
So that now I wonder: would my sons, years from now,
Gather from a tree's silence my own heart's affection,
And in that moment know that once, while I made their world,
I had deeply wished, when they shall have left that world behind,
I would be the tree to their morning?

Toys

Now our boys have such toys
as my brother and I never dreamed;
Did the same spirit stir our make-believe?
Yet outdoor was where we took its measure.

But how could I wish it were otherwise
for them, and would it be wise
since other kids inhabit the same quarry
where X-men wage their fantastic wars?

Indeed we knew the hot spill of blood,
with slingshots searched the bushes and trees,
but also knew ourselves pierced
where the world's songs first were made.

But those video games, those robots,
armaments of glory, sirens of terror,
must root their eyes in our politics
and scavenge for hope in the world's rubble.

Something's amiss, or toys perhaps
have changed their meaning.
In the overflood of their kind,
they've lost their round of seasons.

It may be the same with the world's
weather, but in our time,
there was one season for kites
when the wind seemed to make the sky rounder;

There was another, for marbles and rubber bands,
the earth firmer, the blaze of sunshine brighter;
and yet another, for tops and wheels,
as streetwise we vied for dusty prizes.

      And when the rains came,
and the skies fell with the thunderclap,
how we would run in drenched nakedness
to dare a lightning race to the edge of time.

But how shall I travel to my boys' heart
and break their dreadnought of heroes,
and find, as when light breaks,
the pieces of their manhood whole?

O, their heroes create them,
but if they could invent their games
and stage their future, might they not
surprise the hero with their fate?

A Christmas Story

Papa and Mama were often away the whole day at work and came home late at night. So, after morning school, the twin brothers David and Diego found home like a silent cave. To keep their spirits up as they played, they invented their imaginary sister. She came smiling to them one day, but she would not tell her name. "I shall tell you," she promised, "on Christmas Day."

She had long black hair and her eyes were a deep brown. Her name was secret for it was the source of her magical power. But she refreshed them with visions of a Kingdom hid behind each day's loneliness and fear. Whenever Papa or Mama told them tales of wonder, they understood every word because they had already gone with their sister to those faraway places long ago. "Ah, did I tell you the story before?" Papa would ask. They would laugh then and say, "No, no, but let us hear it again!"

As Christmas drew near, the times grew evil. The armies of the world gathered in a great Desert. Children vanished in a burning mudslide at night. Jeepneys fought in a long, long line to a gasoline station ... And suddenly one morning David and Diego could not call their sister to mind. A silent dragon had come and eaten their dreams so that they could not remember. At times too a giant with a horse's head would thunder over the roof at night. "Ai!" the brothers cried to one another, "what has happened to her? How shall we call her?"

Throughout the year David and Diego had kept saving in a jar all the coins in the house. They knew that at Christmastime, many children would wander door to door caroling with their old tin cans and sticks. "*Ang Pasko ay sumapit* ..." and the brothers would jump, take out as many coins as there were carolers, wait under the bright Christmas Star at the door, and then, after one more carol had been hastily performed, hand out the silvery coin that had waited a year for each caroler. It didn't matter that the same scraggly boy or girl would return night after night.

And so, David and Diego stood every night under their Christmas Star and listened to the unkempt wandering choirs. Sometimes they wondered one to the other, "How shall our sister keep her promise now?" But they would not let anyone know about their secret grief, not even Papa or Mama.

At the first note one night, the brothers rushed to the door and lighted up the welcoming Star. As it shone on the young ragged faces lifted in song, David and Diego almost leaped for joy. For there stood caroling merrily with can and stick, a little girl with long black hair, and her eyes were a deep brown. *O sister!* their hearts cried out, but without words to greet her. They must not let on to anyone in the choir, or the magic would be broken.

The brothers gently touched her hand as they placed two silvery coins there. They asked in silence, and she said in their hearts, *Juli*. The brothers clasped her secret name, and as she joined the other carolers, she glanced back at David and Diego, and her smile told them, "The dragon is dead."

Mama

    Apart, brother, from it being true,
it's cruel still to have to think it,
"That she lives still, breathes, but
is not herself any longer."
But this also is true:
There are new rules, new boundaries,
yet they never were her world
since last a widow's silence tolled ago.
    For instance, now
when her children's children cry,
she must not run to them, nor touch their hurt,
nor gather their tears to her flood,
lest their hardihood she corrupt.
Only when they laugh, tumble about, and build
new worlds to ramble in, and tumble back again,
raucous caucus of twins! – Only then
may she kiss and play with them, let loose
her heart to them, a magic top with still
music of her childhood past.

"You must not worry, Mama …"
is it any use gently to reprove her so?
"Let go, Mama, or this bric or that brac …"
Why? so her eyes grieve. Is Heaven jealous yet
of this bric, that brac one clings to?
O golden airy bricolage! O those warm, happy
pieces of sun's mankindness, bright domicile!

Brother, who laid down that Rule
for the gift of dying –
That when she's happy with nothing,
nor bric nor care, nor brac nor sons,
then only, on that misty peak of nothing,
God shall take her?
Or when your eyes fail, Mama,
or a past text blurs, and things lose their name,
is it time, its slow ravening done?
        Think nothing of it!

It's nothing there, Mama. No thief
hides behind your rocking chair,
no, only a dear absence perhaps yearning
for shape. No ghosts here, now,
where things veil their faces,
where a stray breeze is groping maybe
for a lost rune among your surly roses –
or words perhaps come too late to speak ...
Sleep, Mama, I am by.
Words sound nothing still, and your ghost,
If there be one, is only tomorrow.

I Love You, Girl

I love you, girl, too late, and cannot let go
and think and mock myself, "Fool! ... at your age!"
But here are words and words, for a poem perhaps?
A kind of feeling workout, to see how in their clearing,
as in daylight, to meet such heat as feigns in my blood
a young man's panic and fire on that first fierce night
with his bride, gladly yielding the irrelevant self
to the untouchable sorrow of possession ...

I know no efficiency of action which takes
my passion by its horns, for when I think on it,
it appears an empty brawl, and I begin to mock
again and deny, being too careful of living, taking
no joy in hazard! Yet my blood's hush and roil
is honest as sunlight, and denies its folly;
only its tardiness has made it strange. It passes,
it recurs, a delicious threat of what is possible,
warm tingle of vague infinity,
self's bright, abstract wholeness again ...

Words again, only words! which make the real
unreal yet hold me to that first sorrow
of possession, the same truth now shaken
from the bent tree of my years' tranquil
ordinariness. I must rue that in my mind's
pool of light I deal with you with words
and words that falsify. O, I love you, girl,
too late, but my words must still falsify, because –
because if I kiss you now, girl, I'll be a goner!

'The Book of Embraces'

I'm vexed with myself tonight
that I, fitful tiller of words,
cannot write you a poem,
warm as your ironing-board,
well-shaped like your finest vase,
which should tell everlastingly your truth
clear like any ordinary morning
when the smog lifts to wide-open skies.

What is your truth, or what is love?

Where you move without ripple in my blood,
there the clods of deep little hurts --
oh, forgiven, nameless in memory,
and yet, without my conscious intent,
let to grow like thorny touch-me-nots
and rankly creep with tiny purple eyes
to demean me darkly in my sight.
How their bramble cut my soul
where I would not look to save myself!

Why do I struggle toward your truth?

Where words and words swirl about,
dust in my speech, without power
to trace their meaning in my blood,
I coax like a conscientious gardener
from dead clods their hurtful bloom,
then look upon my soul's wildness
that you had loved, and strain
from our days' erasure of worship,
syllable by syllable,
the struck bliss and dazzle
of our secret 'book of embraces.'

Sestina for the Imp

I no longer doubt, sweetheart, that the world
is ruled by a frolicsome metaphysical Imp
in so many subtle guises, you cannot tell
whether it were your will or a mere accident,
or twist of circumstance, or ghostly chance,
by which something or other consequential
    was accomplished.

You know only years after – by then perfectly
    accomplished –
what the chicken pox ago that quarantined my
    world
had sprung through days of solitude: a lifetime
    chance,
my studious blood meeting up with the fever
    of Imp
where a low-grade passion burned in the accident
of enforced silence and burst its blisters for
    a secret to tell.

What of times past and deep hungers I couldn't
    tell –
other ruins of heart's lusts that had been accom-
    plished,
or fêtes of appetite that relentlessly urged the
    accident –
O, no clear design, only those necessities of a
    self's world
constantly reshaped by underground spirit of Imp
casting dice at leering specters of chance.

I might have been elsewhere lost, for such the
    chance
that winds the time humming and drumming
    to tell
of flights and embraces – spindrift and daze
    of Imp –
by which all feasts and fatalities of desire are
    accomplished;
such, sweetheart, its turns and twists to unfix
    our world
and move its dreamt future to startle of accident.

You will in any event deny purpose in accident,
there only purrs in one's course the engine of
    chance
preparing either rout or routine through which
    our world
is then opened or abruptly closed, to tell
of a truth or delusion already accomplished
long before it were ever possible to trip
    the Imp.

Surprise! even you, sweetheart, are the same
   Imp,
in your person the sweetheart to my pox, by
   accident –
of speech or gesture showing the thing accom-
   plished,
time's most intimate disclosure, not strumpet
   of chance.
How shall fingers work the abacus of desire
   to tell
the stark consummate underlay of your world?

I have no skill to collect the grains of accident,
or subvert chance's ploys, or distract my special
   Imp;
only our netherworlds meet but cannot tell
   the fait accompli.

Country

The Archangel of Gethsemane

The poor families around the plush village of Gethsemane were especially devoted to Gabriel the Archangel, believing that one day he would himself announce the Good News to them and, riding a star like to their Christmas *parol*, lead them out of captivity – as with the Three Kings of old – toward God's own Son, Firstborn of the poor. Fr. Cruz encouraged their faith because it gave them the pure comfort of a delusion.

Throughout the year, the poor kept to their shanties. But at Christmas, their children would go about in random caroling with empty cans and sticks, and on the great day itself of Our Savior's birth, lead their elders in scattered droves over Gethsemane. In full force, husbands, wives, children, relatives poured out into the streets and knocked at the high gates, the children piping "Merry Christmas! Merry Christmas!" as they were taught in school. Their din and insistent music of the doorbell would bring the housemaids down to them, with candies and leftovers, broken toys, old shoes, and clothes – but the times being hard, they preferred even small change, for it was money to hand. Often they went away sad, but hopeful again at the next gate whose huge, intricate *parol* promised a share in the hidden wealth.

This practice provided for years the only link between rich and poor in Gethsemane. But one day, Mr. de Jesus spoke up at the village council: "Let us be honest for once. We give out of fear only, or perhaps, just to be rid of the annoyance. The poor sense this, and press their advantage, for they are sly and laugh at us." Mr. Reyes shook his head: "Fear? What harm can the poor do us? They obey our laws and have no arms." Then Don Emmanuel Pascua observed with a smile: "Despite our laws, we leave these squatters alone. They should return the favor." And so the village council issued a decree that thenceforth the poor should apply at the parish office or a nearby branch of the Ministry of Social Services. Thereby the legal residents could rest and have a tranquil time for themselves during Christmas.

And so it came to pass that in the year of Our Lord 1984, Gethsemane slept in peace for the first time. At the first *misa de gallo*, Fr. Cruz praised the village council for its efficiency. The Great Day of Christmas came and passed without trouble. The streets were deserted and housemaids felt relieved. A few poor families who thought little of decrees were directed to the parish office for hot soup. Only the children of the rich felt oppressed by the day's silence. Knowing nothing of councils or decrees, they became listless at play amidst their gifts from Santa.

As the Great Day ended, a strange event took place that, for fear of ridicule, the press itself censored. Yet it could not be kept secret by housemaids, and soon everyone talked about it, although no explanation could be found.

It seemed that soon after dark, the poor families strode out in procession – husbands, wives, children, relatives, all in their best Sunday clothes, and singing in incredibly sweet voices. O, it was a wondrous sight! Their faces shone with an unearthly glow, not alone from the lighted *parol* that each one bore. And leading the procession was a resplendent figure, his wings about him like a great cloak. His face shone like lightning, and his garments were as white as snow. The rich looked over their gates with fear, but their children ran out joyously into the streets. "Merry Christmas! Merry Christmas." In one breathless moment, the procession vanished in a coruscating wake of stars, and a deathly silence fell upon Gethsemane.

A wild panic then gripped every family. "The children! Where have our children gone?" A great cry of anguish rose up to heaven. But the procession had passed like a dream. Swiftly, frantically, villagers and police raided the shanties. The poor had simply left all their belongings behind – and food on the table, working tools, small change. Not a single soul was to be found. Only dogs wandered about moaning for their lost masters whose smell still lingered in the muddy footpaths and deserted backyards.

Parable of the People

They fled toward sundown, the Minister of War and the King's Second General, and promptly occupied a fort in mid-city with a few hundred troops. Then a commoner went up to the Minister: "How long can you stand a siege? Do you have enough food?" "Our people will give us food," said the Minister and believed it in his heart. "Are you driving away the old despot to assume his own power?" asked another man. The Second General only smiled: "This is a coup de grâce – the people's revolution."

The King laughed aloud when his First General brought him the news. "They have become common rebels," said the King. "Order them to give up this stupidity at once. Let them see that at my word our artillery shall break their every bone."

But the gods had long blinded the King so that he could not see his own people – that all had become rebels. And a widow stood among them and rejoiced over the miracle of conversion. "Yes, a coup de grâce," she said. "For God's own time has come, and I claim the people's victory." (Her husband whom the King feared most, as everyone knew, had been assassinated by secret decree, and the conspirators acquitted in the King's court.)

Then a Prince of the Church raised his shepherd's staff and called out in a loud voice: "Go, brothers, sisters, bring food to the people's fort and torches against the night. Surround the fort with the power of our humanity. The dawn is nigh, mourn no more."

But the King imposed curfew from sundown to morn to cow his subjects, whereupon the people laughed and danced in the streets for they could no longer contain their joy over their freedom. The

King could neither see nor hear. His own Palace had become a prison where his family kept their tears from him – except the Queen who dreamt of a flying ship like a throne and trumpeting angels.

And so the King sent his elite troops in heavy armor under his First General to attack the fort at crack of dawn. "To arms, comrades, to arms!" cried a partisan waving a red flag. "Consecrate our ground with patriots' blood."

"No, brothers, the hour of fire and sword is past," said another man. "Now is our brotherhood forged by our common cross. Our bodies' single barricade shall be the stronger fort."

The crowd wavered in great anguish of soul. The First General sat grim and impassive on his war-machine, and all his cannons pointed at the frightened crowd. "*Aha*! your time is up, disperse!" he thundered. "God has not answered your prayers."

But the people linked their arms, one to the other, strangers all, and stood their ground, calling upon Our Father as His own Son had once taught them. And at that very moment, the faceless and the nameless achieved the singular countenance and identity of humankind; and the soldiers' hearts thrilled to the haunting image of their common nature and brotherhood and sisterhood, and their hands trembled over their guns.

Now another General had been watching from the sky on the King's dreaded flying machines, but when he saw how the people stood up to Death and stunned Death's minions with their offering – food and flowers and prayer beads, and the very body and blood of their humanity – he cried tears and bade his troops land inside the people's fort.

Thereupon, all the people raised a shout to heaven. "Behold!" said the General to his disembarking troops. "The King has become a little brook, and cannot find the sea."

When the King heard the news from the First General, he knew in his heart that he had lost. But his Queen who had steeled her heart against the sweaty mob and heard voices from a Cosmic Hole, turned to him and said: "We must still stand our ground. They are but common rebels. Declare a state of emergency."

"Woman," cried the King in hapless rage, "I must not shed more blood. And if we do, what shall we say in our victory to all others who are spared – or if we lose, to those who may help us escape?"

"O, tell the world again that they were all rebels," said the Queen. "You are the duly constituted power, and the Law is on our side. Do we not read in history, and you said so yourself, that civilization rests on the bones of savages?"

The King bowed his head and wept into his hands. It flashed across his ravaged mind, his heart thrilling with its horror, that he had so perfectly molded his Queen unto his own image and likeness. Like God on the sixth day, he saw his first human creature, but found – alas! for he was only a tired, old king near death – that his creature was compounded from darkness.

That Space of Writing

And when I write, I want the largest space,
Of such breadth, of such length as this world
Never had of forests nor virgin paper,
Where the words never were, their script accursed,
    but only now
               Descending to cry, Freedom!

Then my hands should never feel there were walls
That grow their ominous lichen between my fingers,
Nor my elbows graze the wild beards of rocks
That cathedral my tribe wailing for its god,
    but only now
               Descending without speech!

The words that never were create anew my race,
Their mornings stand clear where ancient skies cascade
Down the singing gorges of the wind. My hands
Draw again the map that alien voyages had wrecked,
    O long ago
               Descending with Cross and Krag!

My elbows swing where rooms void their space,
And I laugh to see the weird syllables of speech
Open their abyss, and stride across the heartland
Of my people's silences where their eyes pour
    like sunlight
               Descending to claim the earth!

O when I write again, the words of any tongue
Shall find no tillage in our blood, nor my hands
Scruple to choke their weed, for first must they bleed
Their scripture in our solitude and yield to our
   scythe's will
                Descending to carve our heart.

The Light in One's Blood

To seek our way of thinking
by which our country is found,
I know but do not know,
for its language too is lost.
To find our trail up a mountain
without a spirit guide –
here is no space where words in use
might stake a claim.

Speaking is fraught with other speech.
Through all our fathers, Spain
and America had invented our souls
and wrought our land and history.
How shall I think counter to the thick
originating grain of their thought?
"I have not made or accepted
their words. My voice holds them at bay."

Look then without words,
nor jump about like ticks
missing their dumb meat.
If there be enough blood yet
in our story for counterpoise,
in speech take no meaning
from elsewhere,
be more thorough than passion.

Whence does one come
when he speaks, his eyes lighting up?
Before speech, all words are dead,
their legends blind.
No one comes from language,
the truth is what words dream.
One speaks, and language comes,
the light in one's blood.

What ravening lions roar
in our blood for our thoughts?
We too have our own thunder
from lost insurrections;
even the present seems a gift,
but mostly unopened.
So much thought is scattered
like grain upon burnt ground.

The soil is ours, and inters
the secret bones of our loss.
We must know our loss, all things
that ghost our time.
Speak now, collect every bone,
lay the pieces together.
Here is true speaking,
a mountain rises beneath our feet!

Is language already given?
– yet we have its use:
a double forgery!
No essences are fixed by words.
Proceed by evacuation
of first seeing; in emptiness
gather the pieces
of breaking light.

No language is beforehand
but its shadow; nothing
in the script, but the other's myth
that now frets your soul.
What breathed there before the words
took their hue and creed?
How, with the same words,
shall another tale be told?

The same words, but not the given,
for void its speech of empire!
Our eyes must claim their right
to our landscape and its names.
What cataract of other minds
has flooded their sight?
We must even fall from our own sky
to find our earth again.

The Dream in the Void

The most of anyone's time is the void,
to it nor words nor memory may find
any route. Void is most, and everywhere,
a treetop stillness loses all thought.
What none remembers has no history,
words only break and cannot speak.
No deed is formed in action without space,
where no suffering is, nor any seed,
nor forgiveness.
          How shall one avoid?

Lord, I prayed, give me myself again, face
without mirror; I know all emptiness,
lone gecko tolling in midnight's gap;
love no longer my solitude where words
run to ground, raising nor hue nor
cry from my stumbling will. Being nothing,
I cannot be filled.
          Lord, where is your gift?

I fell asleep, empty with cries no words
could serve.
       In that void He gave me a dream.
There I stood apart from my childhood's past,
I knew the street, I knew our gate, I looked
without faith. An angry mongrel dog strained
at its leash in our gate. It was Petrel,
but would she know me still? I had my doubt.
Then our door opened, and a tall stranger
came out, and I felt the evening fall. I had moved
closer perhaps, but what I always saw
was scene without motion. I became anxious
for the stranger, yet did not look to see
his face. I simply knew he had no fear.
Petrel barely missed his calf, but I – oh,
it was I had pulled him out of our gate.
Then in anger I turned to that mongrel,
"Why," I said, and the letters of my speech
stood clear in the air, so I could read,
"Why have you not read the books we gave you?"
O I could read their titles as I raged,
there were three, "The Cleanness of the Red Man,"
but two quickly dissolved as I awoke.

I laughed; a silly dream! What could it mean?
If the Unconscious is God, He plays me
a joke!
    I was ten years old in that house,
yet re-entering the dream without words
to speak, I loved that boy who drew Indians
as he listened to the distant thunder
of bison and stealth of mocassined feet.
O Lord, was it then you gave me myself,
and I should love that boy who secretly
wept for them, that they should have lost their land
and he could only draw their vanished trails?
Who are you, stranger? I asked. Then I knew
my father again, taller than silence,
whose words were few, whose love encompassed
so that, without strain, each thing in the void
knew its name, and grew sturdy in stillness,
the center being everywhere – the same treetop
stillness that breathes and quells all thought
of crown or root, nor fears for any leaf.
And Petrel within the gate? – poor mongrel
bitch whose history is no one's book.
O Filipinas! country without speech,
all our words chains, your childhood without past!
What "Cleanness of the Red Man" is offered
if we cannot draw blood from vanished trails
as the lone gecko tolls in midnight's gap?

Jeepney

Consider honestly
this piece of storm
in our city's entrails.
Incarnation of scrap,
what genius of salvage!
Its crib now molds our space,
its lusty gewgaws our sight.

In rut and in flood,
claptrap sex of traffic,
jukebox of hubbub –
I mark your pride of zigzag
heeds no one's limbs nor light.
I sense our truth laughing
in our guts, I need
no words to fix its text.

This humdrum phoenix in our street
is no enigma.
It is a daily lesson of history
sweating in a tight corner.
Its breakdowns and survivals
compose our Book of Revelation.
It may be the presumptive engine
of our last mythology.

Look, our Macho Incarnate,
sweat towel slung round his neck.
He collects us where the weathers
of our feet strand us.
His household gods travel with him,
with the Virgin of Sudden Mercy.
Our Collective Memory, he forgets
no one's fare. Nor anyone's destiny.

See how our countrymen cling
to this trapeze against all hazards.
All our lives we shall be acrobats
and patiently survive.
Our bodies feed on proximity,
our minds rev up on gossip.
We flock in small spaces,
and twitter a country of patience.

Here is our heartland still.
When it dreams of people,
it returns empty to itself,
having no power of abstraction.
Abandoned to itself
and in no one's care,
jeepneys carom through it,
our long country of patience.

Nights I lie awake, I hear
a far-off tectonic rumble.
Is it a figment of desolation
from that reliquary of havoc,
or, out of its dusty hardihood,
that obduracy of mere survival,
a slow hoard of thunder
from underground spirit of endurance?

The Quest

No, I don't think we need fool ourselves
supposing we already have a "national" language:
        Our Constitution only dreams of one,
even temporizes on "official" speech;
our politicians are ever at a loss but,
being sophists, pretend it may be contrived,
and pass laws and juggle an elusive budget;
our academics split the syzygies of syntax
and succeed in confusing most gloriously
one another, bombinating in the void.
        Indeed, we try,
We try, but run counter to our history.

        O desolation of thought!
Our words cannot echo its ghost.
Our own? – but we have none,
their lives have been usurped,
other words have gutted our sight
and made our history. We have no tale
except what they repeat.
We need another power to deflect
their aim or master our own seeing.
But that power isn't in any language
except as we dream the words again.

Or if we have our own words still,
like islands in a stranger's discourse,
we only sense their meanings' drift
as a conch's hollow ocean roar,
but cannot follow in peace.
They no longer bear the chirp of birds
across our sun-steeped land,
nor insect voices on sultry nights
along our secret mountain trails,
for they endure rather an infection
from other meanings that change
the depth and current of their dream.

Just now I spot a wolf spider
on the wall as I write, and see why,
having no web that it can spit out
of its glands, it hunts alone.
    But not so, in our case:
abandoned to silence, we must oppose
our drift and secrete a language to catch
each one's meaning when we meet,
such meaning as we need to carry
our own thought without hurt –
a dying sunlight to the next day's rise.
We begin always with emptiness,
rearrangement of inner ground
by a silent worker beneath the dream.

Balikbayan

Kabayan, it's simply fact, no racial slur,
Pinoy is Filipino, and Kano, American. Such
the national genera, but we mustn't leave it
to diplomacy to trick out their substance or
our prejudice. As we live, neither endures
intrinsic damage nor drift; indeed, we know
we have much of 'the other' too, and no harm,
except that sometimes we have little peace
with our past, I don't myself know why,
as though there were anything to forgive,
as though the past were a separable fate
and we had little will in it. But likewise,
if you chose to be Kano, I should have no call,
by staying there, you did cut clean
though your mind stray here sometimes –
And now that you have returned for a visit,
I kiss you in peace. Welcome!

But to deal with us now –
even as friends from a past we both dearly
cherish, and could have many drinks over,
laughing and crying – you must become
like us with all our faults, our virtues too.
Forgive me, we too see our shortcomings
and need no one's interpreting,
they are part strangely of our wholeness.
We are easily given to laughter,
and San Mig is our national drink,
for that is how we bear with ourselves
and the misery that seems our history;
no, not misery – unless our soul too
were economic – but a lightness of being
as if we've never yet fathomed our pain.

     Perhaps we only see things differently
despite the outward show – highways and malls,
drugs and politics, even our sports and crimes.
We see without concepts, so that our words fail,
and our deeds seem to eschew logic;
we see more with our feelings – not phenomena
but omens, not data but oracles –
for which the mind can establish no grammar.
            Omens and oracles!
O, I exaggerate to stress a different logic,
for laws and rules have less sway with us
than an instinct for decency which like a volcano
lies dormant – in our hearts, where we know
that laws, such as they are in our history, bear
more oppression than justice, serving the interests
of those who have the power and the wealth
and so much more to lose.

In Ordinary Time

    No, kabayan, I don't propose anarchy,
even the Marxists proved totalitarian,
but only respect for each man's difference
which must boil down to an essential dignity.

But have I not said enough?
What more shedding of words and tears ...
          Ah, you smile!
Let us drink to all our ghosts without need
to name them; we're too far out from all
saying, our element besides isn't words only
whose betrayal we need not fear
if our feelings seek no surety from them.
          Mabuhay!

How Our Towns Drown

How in the downpour our towns drown,
downstream of doom to sea we are returned,
houses and pigs in ceaseless procession
as skies boom and fall thundering spears
to beat down all curses and tears to tide –
among seaweed and driftwood and water hyacinths,
prayer-wreaths for the dead and the drowned,

downstream of doom to sea we are returned.
Tottering over manholes, shivering in the blast
of a blind monsoon, its hollow howl
the rolling dreariness of our emptied hills,
our feet doubt their ground where streets
vanish in the gorge and swill of slime –
to flood at last we are flotsam and scum,

houses and pigs in ceaseless procession.
And rushing past our brethren, those lovelorn
cats and cockroaches, amid floating roofs,
lumbering cadavers of cherished scrap,
our naked brats scamper and gambol
over their scavenged loot of murky things,
tires and handbags and bottles and shoes,

In Ordinary Time

as skies boom and fall thundering spears
on Cherry Hill slumping down its slope
and shoveling homes in one boulder swoop –
landfill of families in moaning mud!
so sudden, their screams no echoes bear,
abducted to questioning rage of mind
by what "state of calamity" or "act of God"

to beat down all curses and tears to tide.
Antipolo to Pangasinan the earth rivers
and shoves down Pinatubo's renegade ooze
to our paddies swelling to ocean of muck
and fishponds collapsing to swamp;
for bridges are down, and mountains too far,
to flee and shelter from the water's gore

among seaweed and driftwood and water hyacinths,
what word, what route? what water world
for breathing space, the floors of our dreams
but shiver their fittings and leak their gloom.
Clutch of seaweed for hair,
driftwood for limbs, hyacinths for a cloak,
what new indigene, only survivor to offer

prayer-wreaths for the dead and the drowned?
Requiescant in pace ... vitam aeternam,
so cradle the infant, swaddled in rubble grime,
just now excavated and no mother to hush
its lost wail, no father, no sibling –
surely now their wreck is deaf to cranes
or fingers digging, to what end any change

how in the downpour our towns drown.

My Country's Imp

And we are nowhere still, hostile to process
And living mostly on the surface of things,
Captive to our Imp's metaphysics of happiness –
A spate of all the world's amber mornings.

For we blink the sad, dark faces of things,
The razz and dazzle of our Imp's humor
(Flux of all the world's electric mornings)
Blank time's malice to rouse our spirit's ichor.

O razz and sparkle of our Imp's humor,
Such gristle as shatters the tyrant's laws,
Voids history's ills, and fires our spirit's liquor
Where coups vaporize in politics without clews!

What Imp's grit to scatter the despot's laws!
And because our fathers loved us, their sins fade
Where ventures choke in scams without clews.
Brief triumph! hubbub and rabble of barricade.

And because our kin are loved, their follies fade
Where shanties barnacle our suffocated creeks.
Fleet glory! and baffle and babble retrograde,
Our Imp still rules, and our laughter leaks.

Where our shacks teeter over poisoned creeks,
The thief's our saint who had faith and was saved.
The Imp enthralls yet where our carnival leaks;
But here is no country still, our honchos depraved.

The thief goes scot-free, by a helicopter saved,
The Imp outwits our writ of habeas loot.
No logic avails, no country where lawyers rave,
Everything is soon forgot, all heroics for naught.

Yet our wit is wound with wounds that wail,
Captive to our Imp's metaphysics of happiness.
We bear our fathers' sins ever without bail,
And we are nowhere still, hostile to process.

God

Flying Monk

He was born Giuseppe Desa in Apulia
In 1603.
A strange boy and sickly,
"Open Mouth" his fellows yclept him,
And a Bishop passing by,
Struck by his self-torments,
Idiota fondly described him,
"Of mind not feeble but innocent."
The Capuchins found no place for him
Since he could not concentrate;
But not long after, the Conventuals
Took him as their stable boy,
And at 22, by a fluke at the finals,
He became a Franciscan,
And bread and wine could consecrate.
One day, after Mass, he floated among the candles
And, unburned, flew back from altar
To a pew, while his flock wondered
If the holy goose had wings?
This was his sole accomplishment;
He would dance and fly
Because the sky was a clear blue,
But never knocked a candle down
Nor broke a twig from a tree.
He danced with a friendly monk in air
And cured a madman above his ground.
At 60, he died afloat
As he listened intently to unheard choir.

He flew; it could not be doubted.
Even Leibnitz watched,
And Dingwell, archskeptic,
Could only say, "Our knowledge is yet inadequate,"
And shake his head.
What need to fit to mental construct
An indigestible fact?
The Duke of Brunswick, another witness,
Became a Roman Catholic,
But Giuseppe's is not intellectual belief.
He had little mind, only delight.

God of Our Youth

Introibo ad altare Dei
Qui laetificat juventutem meam.

Yes, Al,
It's quite sad to stand tall as weeds
On the plain of idling talk,
The God of our youth banished –
                But we seem now
To insist on it as mind stalls
On a late fantastic hurt,
Unseasonable yearning.
    Of course,
This may be a passing mood
Beneath talk toward sunset,
Even as the mountain, I'm told,
Continues to rise beneath our feet.
    We pass
To topics as we please,
And think we understand,
                And yet,
Do we ever know our mind,
That volcanic mound from where
    our words come?
What strange fury may be veiled
By memory's cirrus about its dormant
    mouth!

            But yet again, hold —
Is this not medieval talk?
A time ago, did we darkly know,
Or was it at all knowledge?
            Yes, as far back
As mind has words for,
We knew, and had a way,
But the words were Latin ...
                      All haze as gold
Dust now in the late sun's flood
Where we stand, bored with lip service,
Where liquor and women offer ease
Without need for words more.
We choke on the magical rubric
And could perhaps weep in private
As men do when they lose their grip
   on action.
      Under the circumstances,
Speech is of course difficult,
Our words shape nothing definite;
It must be a matter of standpoint.
                  But we might note
The prosaic in our words' enclosure,
Its possible worth:
The days of our youth are romanticized
For present need —
A heart's bypass, as it were,
For reason of health.
      We may need to adjust
To mountain air of higher talk,
Like, say, the metaphysics of nostalgia,
Or the care of time,
Prolific and versatile.

                    Because the angel
Of memory bars the cave,
Flaming kris in hand,
Where the God of our youth rests in peace,
We must find another route
Past his dusty tomb.
          Consider his silence.
At cloud-parting,
When we least expect eruption,
A sudden peak could heave into view
And we would not have the words
To believe.
                    But yet, since our talk
Has chanced upon his tomb
And did not trouble his sleep with tears,
We could attempt the airy climb
And not fear lest strange voices
Hurl us back
Where time cocoons our youthful love.
We must remain content without revenge
For strangulation of familiar speech.
It is with words that we woo God,
We have no other means.

Parable of the Andromedan

"Come no closer," the boy heard the Voice in his head rather than with his ears. "Speak no words, for your thoughts are like a clear brook."

The Voice was strangely sweet and brought a deep sensation of peace. Its wonder was that the boy seemed to understand much more than the words that he formed to receive it. Yonder whence the Voice streamed, a silvery sphere hovered above the century-old acacias along the town plaza. His playmates had been called home for the Angelus, but he lingered by the ruined gate with his kite that all afternoon had proudly soared in the cool, windswept sky. After the church bells' tolling, nature suddenly fell into a deep hush, and it seemed that into the darkening space the sun had spun a great whirling top which had absorbed its dazzling light. And down its pointed tail there glided a tall creature – like a dragonfly! standing upright, its four iridescent wings quivering in the air.

I must only be dreaming. But oh, if I had such a kite!

"I'm as real as your dragonfly, but you must not touch me. My element is like your sun."

What is 'element'?

"As earth to earthworm, or air to bird."

Where is your home?

"A great beautiful planet with four rings around it. You would think it were Saturn, but it is in the constellation you call Andromeda."

Andromeda?

"So your astronomers call that vast field of stars."

You know our earthworms and dragonflies. Your own home must be like ours. What is your name?

"Our world is very different from yours, but I cannot describe it with your words. We have no names; we have no need for words. It is enough to see, don't you agree? Looking is a doorway to the house of thought."

O, I can look and see around me, but I don't know what others have studied ... there are so many names! How did you know earthworms and dragonflies if you don't have them?

"Ah, how shall I begin to tell you! All thought is spread out in the universe like your sky. When you think, it isn't really with words; the words come later to help you remember. Your thoughts are the heartthrobs of all life in the universe awakening in your mind."

Did you see me before you came?

"I knew from afar that you were lingering here to watch the stars march out, and trace the outlines of gods, heroes, and animals from your mythology. How I wish you could follow me ... you are but a child still, and your mind is very clear, there aren't so many names yet! All the stars in your sky speak at night, but no one listens."

Will you take me then to Andromeda?

"You would not be able to come back here. Dumanjug by the sea, acacias purpling in summer, your brother Nene and his treasure-trove of comics and marbles ... A thousand years shall pass, your sun shall have set forever, and you would still be young, there would be no one to return to."

Why did you come? Did you lose your way in the dark?

The Voice fell silent. Its great diaphanous wings became very still. And the boy felt such awe that for a frightful moment, it seemed the ground had opened and he was falling, falling sheer among countless shooting stars. Then the wings whirred and glowed with soft, ethereal iridescence.

"I have not lost my way, I have only traveled a very great distance. Of all dwelling-places among the stars, your Earth is the most blessed. I'm here to visit with the Child whom you call Jesus."

Ay, naku! you're very late. There were three kings from the East, Melchor, Gaspar ... but that was very long ago.

"Ah, but He's here, for He became like you. He took your element so that you may also be like Him. Don't you see? – that is the secret and miracle of change."

O poor dragonfly! He died a long time ago, didn't you know? Then he rose again ... and then his close friends went about informing everyone, and so we still remember ...

"Please, I'm no dragonfly ... But you say that He rose again from the dead! That is your key, and you must thank His friends for remembering. It should be obvious ... only time passes."

But we all die, and people may not even remember our names.

"You will rise again and thank death for the passage. Here too at last, after a long voyage, I yearn for that passage. Upon this ground I do not only know what all of us in Andromeda know, here I feel all Being. Your St. Paul says, 'I live in Him.' Surely you know what I speak of, although people call Him by many names – God, Brahma, Allah, Manitou, Bathala."

We know only names of things. And words sometimes are troublesome.

"Most men by the time they're older, and their hearts colder, no longer know the great unspeakable wonder of it. He walked among you, His own feet blessed this Earth! He talked and ate with you, and left His own words with you – speech and fables he adopted from your way of speaking and storytelling, that you may always remember and be like Him!"

But memory is full of tricks. People are always arguing about their opinion on anything.

"Oh such frail vessel is human memory! Either its pure water is spilled from too much shaking, or it grows stale from neglect. Let your proud words fall away; drink rather from His memory."

The Voice modulated into Song, without words but deeper than all possibility of meaning, and ineffably sweet. Then a dazzling vision filled the boy's mind: All things are calm, for they know their nature; all things are bright, for they are transfigured. O holy night!

Suddenly, in a twinkling of blinding light, the Andromedan vanished. And looking up, the boy saw beneath the moon's bright scimitar a shooting star. Joy to the world! his heart leaped as he ran home. He heard the wandering carolers' songs on his street. Peace on earth, he repeated after them, to all men of good will. But would not his parents now be angry with him for coming home so late? That ripple of anxiety quickly dissolved in a deep flood of peace. He heard again in his heart the Andromedan's sweet gentle voice. *All the stars in your sky speak at night, but no one listens.*

Parable of the Tent People

The Royal Physician had vehemently denied that the King was in the last stages of a rare psychic disorder called Werewolf's Syndrome. But the King's subjects, anxious about their children's future and threatened by a warlike commune in the hills, clamored for a long-forgotten tradition called the People's Will. The Royal Court consulted with the King and ruled, despite the Queen's premonitory dreams and tears, that a General Election be held.

Now there was at that time a small community of workers without work and peasants without land who had put up tents on a rich man's property. Day and night they fasted and prayed to One whom they called Our Father, and prayed and fasted to find again the free and happy country that, because they were poor and ignorant, they had lost to the tyrant King and his sycophants. And people passing by in the street wondered about the strange peace that hovered over that encampment of the poor and powerless. They were in fact moved to tears by that peace which in their hearts they craved but could not think possible in deprivation. After work, they would join the Tent People for prayers and savor again in silence the sweet peace that enveloped them. Some brought food and clothing for the Tent People's children.

And so it came to pass that, when the Tent People heard about the Election, they prayed even for the King and his Queen, and since they had no experience in government and politics, they pleaded with the One whom they called Our Father to protect the People's Will.

The day before the Election, the King bled from both his hands, wetted involuntarily his purple robes, and then fell into a coma, although both his eyes would not close. And thus the Queen, who had carefully prepared for this minor disaster, stood in the King's place for election. The King's counselors and generals assured her of victory. The people, they said, are too ignorant and too miserable for anger over the deception; besides, fraud, bribery, and the force of arms at the places of election would surely thwart their will.

It was the King's last deception. His eyes, even in his dying condition, could yet see all the things that were taking place, but he could not speak. An unendurable stench filled the Palace which all the Queen's perfumes could not quench. Since all his life had been a lie, at last even language abandoned him. All his supporters turned away from him without a word.

An inexperienced widow whose husband had been treacherously murdered on the King's secret orders, was acclaimed by the people at all places of election, except at those ghostly precincts where the Queen won. People danced and embraced each other in the street, and waved a thousand yellow flags, as the widow, simply dressed and without make-up, joined the Tent People to thank and glorify the One Who is called Our Father. There, among the poor and powerless, the widow forgave the Queen who had reviled her, and all the people lifted up their voice in one great shout of joy, *Vox populi, Vox Dei!*

Why I Believe

I have never yet doubted, sir, but
in later life acquired the strangest reason why,
between every space where nothing is,
I should hold converse with His vanishing
spoor. Or is it perhaps just so,
that one's stories He might spin clear
off gore and grime, humus and hue,
to the least twig of that fractal branching
of one's graveward plot? But how often
I lack for words to tell those secrets I store
without alphabet and that crush my soul.
If they were my plot, how should I be sure
my parts would hang together, or that
their end, that last lightning part, would
compose fine enough weather?

In Ordinary Time

O, those myriad lives past, those nameless
faces in crowds, sir, that hurry past,
how unthinkable each bliss, each grief
that none remembers! Was it the rain, say,
voided those lovers' incurable longing, or
a sigh suspended from a moonstruck trellis
invited them to kiss and embrace? O,
in which part of the river on a Sunday spree
did the happy lover drown? Tell us, tell us,
for we live still, still partaking of mysteries
they have endured. Is there no text can hold
wisp of their hair, dust of their bones?
no epitaph, no shard of a moment's fevered
cry, to compose in few syllables a least
hint of their once passionate breath?
If none, the living were mere oppression!
What greater malice, sir, than to be,
and impassioned, dwindle to a nothing,
stone-deaf score to a quavering note.
Who listens yet when one has passed?
Aye, one's words are common speech –
mass burial of lives in ordinary time,
that vast memory no liturgy redeems.

Yet, sir, it isn't that I would pry,
no, there may be novels enough to read
with even our choir of texts sputtering about
that futhark sticking in deconstructionist throat.
The certainty undecidable is what gives peace,
that beyond every name, in Someone's mind
whose dance is our text's despair,
all one's fictions are justly tolled.

Forever Advent

We gather every Sunday of Advent
and talk and prophesy
as we light each candle.
      How our sons and daughters
have grown with our country's ills!
Shall they perhaps invent
from their games and griefs
a hagiography for our people's bereavement?

For us, it is forever Advent,
a long coming, a long hunger.
Our words speak beneath their ashes.
Is it yet possible, at this late hour,
out of the heart's cold and waste,
to be in touch with that first wonder?

By what compass or dream shall one
set out through the hours' fall and plunder
to kiss that dead star's light?
      In what aching mote of sun
or slow and rear corrosion of void?

We must speak to that first death,
or perhaps, more wisely, forbid
speech to weave its amber brede,
let silence and its long fermenting
distil the ancient creed.

Neither fish has swum that distance
nor songbird sung of its lonely tract,
yet there in that waste of dread
must each go uncompanioned,
with neither scrip nor staff,
and an empty sky his rack.

Listen, but form no syllables
for the thunder of its wild lament,
its flesh outcast in starlit manger.
No angels trumpet that far-off light,
no shepherds gossip of dogstar or child,
no virgin maid nor young dreamer by her
    nor mate.
    None, and in our heart's cave
a king's gift smoulders without speech.

Is it forever Advent?
And when all four candles have been lighted,
shall the year toll again for unborn babes,
and our hunger creep through its labyrinth?
    O to grasp but frailest reed
of hay from an empty crib!

Old Shepherd Joachim

Together with the other shepherds, old Joachim found the child and its parents in a stable, just as the angel had told them. The stable lay in darkness and looked abandoned. Because it was unsightly and smelled of dung and animal fodder, it was set apart from the only caravanserai in Bethlehem.

The child's mother who was called Mary and her young husband Joseph were very much surprised to see the shepherds coming out of the dark. But Joachim stepped forth and greeted them. "We have come to see your child about whom we were told by an angel." Joseph looked toward Mary by the manger, and she smiled her welcome to the shepherds.

The child lay in the manger, wrapped in swaddling clothes, for the night was very cold. The shepherds, finding space among some cattle sleeping on their feet, looked on the child with great wonder. For the angel's words shone for them like a torch in the dark. "Do not be afraid," the angel had said, "I bring you news of great joy to be shared by all the people. Today in the town of David a Savior has been born to you."

Joachim wept for joy. Never had he felt such strange happiness. He saw again that flood of ethereal light which bathed the hills and heard again the heavenly host singing beyond all human music. "Glory to God in the highest and on earth peace to all men of good will." He knelt on the straw-covered ground and pondered in his heart what it all meant.

'O, who can understand this marvel? Has the Lord my God chosen to dwell with us in just this form – a human child, so helpless and poor like us? Why? All men desire wealth and power and a great name for immortality. And here is God to save us! by what means? A child is but a wee creature, naked, and must be cared for. Even now Herod must think it foolish for any god to desire to be like us. What descent to our flesh and its frailties! What decrease in power to attract men's admiration and following!'

So Joachim revolved the thoughts that became the tears in his old eyes as he looked on the baby in the trough. All the shepherds were silent, but their faces shone with joy as though they had journeyed a long distance and were come at last to a great plain of abundant pasture.

'As the angel foretold, we have become the bearers of glad tidings to all the people.' So Joachim pursued his thoughts. 'To think that in our lonely fields, in this stable among beasts of burden, we are the very first to know and look on the world's Savior, we who have no wealth but our sheep and children, and are helpless before our rulers, and when we die, have no monuments to our names. But tonight, we adore this Child. How have we found God's mysterious favor? This Child is the Christ! In my heart I believe and rejoice.'

As the shepherds made to leave, a star burst and stood still like a great lantern that swathed the hills in a soft gentle light. All looked up in awe, and Joachim cried out in a trembling voice. "Oh, blessed are the poor and those without power and name. They have nothing to hold them to the world where other men think to satisfy their desires, where the heart breaks without God. They have nothing, and so are free in their hearts and ready to receive Him."

The shepherds were glad that Joachim had spoken for them. As they bade Joseph and Mary good-bye, the star shone as though the angel who had first appeared to them were now that star – the angel of memory by which their faith might forever burn.

The Blind Shepherd

"Surely, they were angels," said Joshua, the blind shepherd, "for never have I felt such joy as when I heard their hosannas."

Abel gazed on his brother with pity. "Oh, Joshua, tonight a new world was born because the heavens opened and all God's angels came down to worship Him on earth."

"Tell me about the angels. How many were they? Did they fly about like blinding suns with great wings?"

"You couldn't count them if you could look without fear or if their splendor were less dazzling. But where I crouched behind our flock and shaded my eyes with both my palms, they looked like ourselves but clothed in God's own resplendent light."

Then Joshua wept. "Never have I seen any light. Only the words I hear shine with their message, but my eyes can never shape the beauty of their form."

Abel embraced his brother to lighten his grief. "Let us follow the angels' message and go to Bethlehem."

They joined the other shepherds who led their flocks to a temporary sheepfold. But their father Isaac, who was the chief elder of their little community, came to the two brothers and said: "Stay here, Abel, with your brother, and watch over our sheep. Everyone wants to see this thing that has happened which the Lord has made known to us."

Abel placed his arm around Joshua and watched the other shepherds disappear over the hill. "Tell me again," said Joshua, "what the angel who first appeared said to them."

So Abel, with tears that his brother could not see, recalled the glory of that night. "When the angel came like the morning sun over the hill, we were all terrified, but he said, 'Do not be afraid, I bring you news of great joy to be shared by all the people. Today in the town of David a Savior has been born to you. He is Christ the Lord, and this is a sign for you. You will find a baby wrapped in swaddling clothes and lying in a manger'."

As he was speaking, Joshua jumped and his face lighted up. "Look," he said, pointing to the sky. A comet flashed across that immense void of darkness and then stood still like a star whose brightness made a luminous plain cloud upon cloud.

"Oh Joshua, can you see?" cried Abel, with fear in his heart. "It is indeed a star that shines there, and its light tonight is the glory of Bethlehem."

Joshua shouted and danced for joy. "Brother, brother, I see with both my eyes!" And the two brothers hugged each other and danced around their sheep. But then Joshua suddenly stopped, trembling, and a strange look of pain came into his eyes. "I see more – more! My heart breaks for joy, but a great sorrow also chills it, because I see, and no darkness veils the things to come."

"Joshua, now it is your turn to tell me, for my eyes only see the new world that is born tonight."

"Love has entered the world and made it new; its mystery is beyond words but fills our hearts with hope and peace. I see three kings from the East traveling in a desert, bearing gifts for the Child in Bethlehem. I see another king, but he is wicked, many infants will die because of him. Beauty and terror seem inseparable in our world."

And then Joshua wept and his brother could not comfort him. "The Baby in the manger – I see a dark shadow across it, it is His cross! Oh, He can save us only through His death, and no peace nor joy shall last until people learn how to forgive their enemies in their hearts. But for the human heart, there is no heavier terror than the need both to give and to receive forgiveness."

Both brothers sat on the ground in silence. They watched the star shining steadily on Bethlehem.

Casaroro Falls

Our instincts on holiday urged a walk
through the countryside, a brief jungle trek
as lightsome quest to fill a vacant hour.
No, we didn't think that bruited marvel,
cliff's fall of waters pouring from the sun!
was too far to walk or too hid to find –
but no longer young, my wife and I did
worry about our sons, although they were
as sure-footed as mountain goats and spry.

Resting awhile in a wild little glade
throbbing with the noonday whirr of crickets,
we quenched our thirst with bottled sun-warmed Sprite.
With shouts as to dare the encroaching woods,
our boys leaped to the clearing's sunlit edge –
the mountain received them without a sound!
I sprang after them, and gripped my wife's hand
as the sun blanked her sight where her heart dropped,
Oh, where? – our boys had found their hearts' mountain!
But we who knew danger and kept her speech,
must track that sheer drop without syllable,
foot to crevice, hand to vine, butt to earth,
eyes yearning to see the roaring waters
of her text – in full flood, naked to view,
in the vast sounding wilderness around.

Ai, here is no time, and the sun hangs fire –
and we are lost, and cannot ever speak.
Our hearts cry fear in the desolate woods
fraught with accident, and cry, *Where is God?*
or His hand if bush to grip free its root,
or vine to cling to grow a row of thorns.
O, how far down our cliff yet?
                                    A rumor
of waters drifts up to taunt our hearing
as we hang from the crumbly slope and slide
our bodies down the trail that slips and twists
like a coil of gut through the tangled shrubs;
any loose rock may suddenly cry out
and rain down stones and earth at last to break
the stillness made the tangled forests wild
and the cliffs hang sheer.
                            Our bodies pressed so
to earth must sense the weird geometries
of breath and sweaty grip, postulating
in grime a sudden precipice to flesh.

Through the jumble of fern and thorny vine
we glimpse a shimmer of stream far below,
tumble of rocks like rugged cuneiform
to the dead tumult of the mountain's birth.
The falls sound everywhere her murmurous
thunder, but invisible, cascading
without alphabet through the heave of trees
and fall of vines; amid the surge and roar
of waters, the derelict boulders seem
to fill the tidal caverns of her sound.

Our boys wait a long time for us, laughing
wet and bold on the stream's tilting boulders;
the waters swirl barbaric round their feet
and toss up glinting spindrifts of the sun.
They wave to us like spirits of the woods
and point to the falls proclaiming her name,
                    And we look
to see her descending nude from her cliff,
and shield our eyes from the dazzle and sheen,
utter tumult and panic of her name –
        Casaroro! wild oceanic tongue
to the mountain's cliffs of cool greening dusk.
Our boys must know what haunts her troubled speech,
from innocence and wonder they suppose
half the world's seas thundering down from God's
open hands, but I – dimly, through the lush
stillness of forests sprouting wild from earth –
I sense how the earth will last long after
our boys have become men and forgotten
how once a mountain strode tall through their speech.
                    And again I look –
a stark foreboding of our flesh's tumble
shivers my faith, and plucks in strange despair
a fierce conjecture from God's thundering plunge.
Was it death's steep annihilating drop
invented our God? or tendril of hope
that in our own cliff's fall to His wet sod
should sprout a deep abounding wilderness,
Casaroro around His streaming hands.

Loam, Azure, Salt

Lord God, Word Alive,
Let fall from us all our words,
Cumulus of pride, ash of despair;
Be silence of earth, sky, sea,
Our vestment and prayer now.

Where breath and act
Stand wordless and clear, may our lies
Lose their script, and grieving Nature
Find again, in that void we call Self,
Your Word – loam, azure, salt.

Be Your Word, apart,
The stillness of our suffering world:
Parchment of our wounded Earth, scroll
Of our moaning Sea, screed of our yearning
    Sky –
O, ours still, as victim, as gift!

Where are the syllables
To sound the gorges of our greed?
Where the flaming writ to scour
Stark deserts of our desire?
Where the letters to forge our creed?

O teach us again,
Natives without speech in Your Word,
Both text and deed of our Communion —
Wine of twilight in our mouth,
Blood of sunset through our heart.

Afterword

What for Me a Poem Is

I was asked, What is a good poem? – I think something made up of words is a poem, or it isn't; when it is a poem, it is good. One can always tell when one has really been moved by many poems in his or her reading life. There is no hard-and-fast definition of the poem because the poem is always work of imagination, and the imagination has infinite possibilities of form. Wallace Stevens in "Modern Poetry," 1942, speaks of "The poem of the mind in the act of finding/ What will suffice. ... It has to be living, to learn the speech of the place./It has to face the men of the time and to meet/The women of the time."

The imagination is the finest form of intelligence, and so, the poem is "of the mind." In the choice of the right words in the right order so as to give one possible form to an experience, in full consciousness of it, one finds "what will suffice." "It has to be living": the poet's experience, be it a feeling or sense impression, a train of thought, or an incident, is now, as poem, flesh become word. I have always thought that words have their meanings, not from their differential relations so much as from life, or a moment, lived. Such meanings are not themes or ideas or abstractions (as in most analyses or interpretive readings of poems); they are values of the imagination, they impart the very sensation and rhythm of living. That moment of intense living is the poem: the very words come alive, as in "emerald/ stone-unripe guavas pack their smell of iron" (Nick Joaquin); or "I have not grown a clove of hearts/To mourn the multitude of her going" (Amado L. Unite); or "He grudged the clutching mollusk its involuted stores,/Pried, that the pearly oyster part its scrupulous doors" (Edith L. Tiempo). For the reader also, the poem is to live.

The making of the poem has "to learn the speech of the place." If we write in English, it is our English – our own clearing in that medium; it is our own way of inner speaking in our own place (our history, our politics, our natural surroundings, our customs and cuisines). Inner speaking, because it is the mind seeking and finding "what will suffice." Then such a poem, once made, can "face the men of the time" and "meet the women of the time." *To face*: to confront, to come to terms with; *to meet*: to engage, to hold easy and intimate converse with. Upon our own ground, in our own place and time, from one consciousness to another – an inner dialogue. "I would meet you upon this honestly," says the poet (or the poem's speaker) to his reader; and "I too would meet you upon it as honestly," says the reader to the poem's speaker.

Let me elaborate. The lyric poem gives body or form to a human voice. There is a speaker, a persona of the poet, who speaks through the poem and lives only in the poem. The lyric speaker always tells a story – the story of a moment lived: a mood, an observation, a stance. "Get real," Franz Arcellana tells writers. It is often the case, I should think, that in the poem's imaginary moment the poet is most real to himself; that is to say, the writing of it was the very living – all of his life-experience finds, as it were, a still point of meaningfulness in the poem's imaginary moment.

That the poem's imaginary speaker is one singular human voice affirms what all lyric poetry celebrates – the integrity, the autonomy of every human being (despite all philosophical or ideological negation), and so, the premium value of each one's experience of living. In the poem's own living moment of speech – if only there – one human being is alive, free, and whole, through his own personal anguish, through her own personal rapture.

That word *experience* is from Latin *experiri*, a word associated with faring, going on a journey, attempting, with peril and fear: one goes forth, one tries and is tried, one meets with chance and sudden danger, and nothing is sure. That isn't the meaning but rather, the meaningfulness of the word *experience* – in historical time (the poet's life course) and imaginary (the time of writing). Experience is our only point of immediate contact with reality whose element or weather is mystery: immediate, with all our bodily senses and (when we are blessed) in full consciousness of mind and feeling. It is at that point of contact where one feels and sees and knows (perhaps). That is the insight, a seeing and knowing within the experience: illumination of a thought that no idea expresses, a radiance of feeling that no thought catches. That insight is what gives rise to the poem. One lives and can make oneself fully aware of the living, the experience. The making oneself aware is part of the effort of writing the poem.

The meanings of words arise not from the words themselves but from lives lived. This is why we speak of a living language, or why language is labile and dynamic, always transforming and even transcending itself through its evocative power, as in imagery and metaphor. The common usage of language is the common living of people speaking and thinking in that language in their own place and time. Language is the community of the living, and so, it is never static; a people or a culture dies with its language. And so, also, through each one's own place and time, the dictionary meanings of words, and the meanings that are shaped by grammatical categories and rhetorical devices, are fundamentally approximations of the meaningfulness of moments that are lived in an *individual's* experience in his own community. Community itself achieves reality through faith in the imagination of its writers, thinkers and scholars; that faith assimilates their imagination, a process of assimilation about which we might adopt Shakespeare's scintillating words in Ariel's song –

> Of his bones are coral made;
> Those are pearls that were his eyes:
> Nothing of him that doth fade,
> But doth suffer a sea-change
> Into something rich and strange.

So then, in and through that common language, its living human community breathes; but in and through the poem's language, an individual voice sounds which insists upon its own integrity. For the poem's language itself is work of imagination.

As said earlier, when we read or write a poem, we have to do with the meaningfulness of a moment that has been lived. The words of the poem are signposts of that meaningfulness: by their very sounds and interrelations, their order and rhythm, they create a path through language that leads to a clearing where the meaningfulness of a human event or a human condition touches our own humanity. This is what it means to be moved by a poem: we have entered someone's experience and grasped our own humanity. That is what we mean when we say, "the poem is to live."

Let us go back to the idea of form. I said earlier that the poem's words give a body or form to a human voice. That voice is what we hear when we read a poem. That the artifact – the thing made up of words – gives a possible form to a human event is all that the maker or poet can claim; only a possible form because, as regards that event, or similar experience, there are always other possible ways of giving it a form: "a mouth, a way of happening" (W. H. Auden). Every poem is, as it were, an imaginary enactment of a human affair or concern.

Its verbal form is simply the external format and shape of the poem on the page: the physical text. But the inner form of the poem is essentially abstract, it can only be conceived in one's mind from the poem's words. The poet, and later the reader, *imagines* the ongoing process and the final pattern of the event or experience as someone – the speaker or observer in the poem – has lived through that event or experience. Of course, we have to understand the words of the poem and catch the intent of the poem's rhetorical figures and devices. But the poem's words and figures are only the flesh, as it were, of a moment that has been lived; that living of the moment, in the poem, is its soul, the poem's inner form.

But was not that moment of intense living only imagined when the poem was wrought? And what, indeed, will suffice?

Yes, only imagined; the moment has passed. What the poet remembers, at the time of writing, is often only a fragment of what has been lived, without word yet: an elusive ghost of something that has already happened. But, you may well ask, what was that moment that promised the fruit of living in full consciousness of itself, that held the crown of being real again to one's own self? What has happened? – An event *only in the poet's consciousness*, be it only a thought or a stance as yet wordless, without definite form, where he seems to have grasped something of his own reality, that reality which, for anyone, can only be the living, from moment to moment, albeit it is irremediably the case that the living, in full consciousness of it, is rare. That event which now spurs the poem's writing may also be something long resident in the poet's timeless unconscious from which it has been fetched – like live coal from its ashes – by a word that came unbidden, a sudden memory, a personal encounter, an incident witnessed or read, a face in the crowd, whatever else in the poet's present course of living. Indeed, the poem may well be a constellation of such events: as it were, their living anew.

Now, if the poet pays heed, what he wants to apprehend is not meaning, as in a definition, but meaningfulness. *Something*: a meaningfulness that flickered there and vanished; *there*: a place as yet without description, as also a moment before it passed, before any possible speech. That living fragment or seed, if you will – a pulse of sensation, a motion of feeling, a spark of thought, a word perhaps or even a line on offer – propels the poem-of-it, where *it* is the unspoken moment. So now the writing of it demands that the moment be imagined. For what is most real is what is most imagined. The poem is the moment spoken for.

And what will suffice? – Always, what suffices is the meaningfulness of a moment that has been fully lived because fully imagined.

I have been speaking so far about the poem on a general plane from the perspective of its writing (and its reading, as though one were writing it). By way of a conclusion, I might say a few words about our writing in English.

It need hardly be pointed out that in our country's history since the American colonial regime, English is as much lingua franca as Tagalog or Cebuano; when today we speak Cebuano (or Tagalog or that evolving called "Filipino"), notice how often English infiltrates it, in the same way that through the centuries Spanish has occupied regions of its sense and sensibility. Incidentally, when our students fail their grammar and composition in English or "Filipino," or read works in those languages with little comprehension, I believe that what fails is their *sense for language*: it does not really matter which language; lacking that *sense*, what words and sentences they read are already dead in the water.

I would go further and assert that, because our education and reading is in English (and translations into English), we have also, unconsciously, adopted (though not in any absolute sense) its forms and categories so that its way of thinking deeply influences the way we make sense of our experience; yet, we are not its subjects and prisoners, for we have in turn colonized it, as it were. When we write in English, we write conformably to its grammar and syntax, but find our own voice because our meanings are drawn from our response to our own time and scene. If our response is shaped by the language we employ, so is the language molded to our need to engage critically with our own historical scene and circumstances; *critically*, from the Greek word *krinein*, to divide (sift, discern) and to judge, which yields the English words, *crisis* and *criticism*. What if that engagement were already determined (though never in any absolute sense as to make us all robots) by genes and gender, by social class and education, by ideology and paradigm, by our history and culture? Our writing brings to a crisis (to a point of division and judgment) our thoughts and feelings, and we *come* literally *to terms* with our own circumstances. So then, it wouldn't be right to privilege one over the other; both human response and language are crucial for the poem's making, but ultimately, what moves poet and reader is the poem's subject, that which has been lived and *imaged* to mind or consciousness again (for the poet, "ghost guessed" in the making; for the reader, already formed, performed, interpreted). The imaginative work is not so much written *in* a given natural language as wrought *from* it. Wrought in *verses*, turnings of language, *furrows*: for the poet is tiller of the soil of language. As the tree to its ground, so the imagination to its words.

Needless to say, not all poems have their name and habitation in a specific locality: a particular country, or people, or culture; not all poems are, specifically, "American" or "Canadian," "Tagalog" or "Ilocano"; they may well transcend such historical boundaries and fictions and take on, as it were, all humankind because their meaningfulness stays on a general and abstract plane: the lyric speaker speaks as one human being to another. That is the supreme fiction made real. (I bear in mind that, curiously, we speak of a certain field of study and imaginative energy as "the humanities," suggesting for me that what we call "human qualities and attributes" still unravel their mystery.) So, be the poem's language American English or Bulacan Tagalog, nationality or regional identity may be superfluous. If the poem has "markers" of locality – "junipers," say, or "azucena" – they do not necessarily ground the poem in some "native clearing." Which, of course, is not to say that there aren't poems whose subject and style may announce what the poet Fernando Maramág calls our own "scene so fair"; and we might begin to have a sense for it – if the poem does appear to move toward it – from simply knowing who its author is. What truly matters for both poet and reader is what his or her imagination owes its allegiance to.